CREATE
IN ME
A HEART
OF
MERCY

Books from (in)courage

DEVOTIONALS

Take Heart: 100 Devotions to Seeing God When Life's Not Okay
Empowered: More of Him for All of You

TRADE BOOKS

The Simple Difference by Becky Keife
Come Sit with Me

BIBLE STUDIES

Courageous Simplicity: Abide in the Simple Abundance of Jesus
Courageous Joy: Delight in God through Every Season
Courageous Influence: Embrace the Way God Made You for Impact
Courageous Kindness: Live the Simple Difference Right Where You Are

Create in Me a Heart of Hope
Create in Me a Heart of Peace
Create in Me a Heart of Wisdom
Create in Me a Heart of Mercy

For more resources, visit incourage.me

AN
(in)courage
BIBLE STUDY

CREATE IN ME A HEART OF MERCY

Dorina Lazo Gilmore-Young and the (in)courage Community

Revell
a division of Baker Publishing Group
Grand Rapids, Michigan

Published by Revell
a division of Baker Publishing Group
Grand Rapids, Michigan
www.revellbooks.com

Printed in the United States of America

Library of Congress Cataloging-in-Publication Data
Names: (in)courage (Organisation)
Title: Create in me a heart of mercy / (in)courage.
Description: Grand Rapids : Revell, a division of Baker Publishing Group, [2023]
Identifiers: LCCN 2022034074 | ISBN 9780800738150 (paperback) | ISBN 9781493438785 (ebook)
Subjects: LCSH: Mercy—Textbooks.
Classification: LCC BV4647.M4 C74 2023 | DDC 241/.4—dc23/eng/20220907
LC record available at https://lccn.loc.gov/2022034074

23 24 25 26 27 28 29   7 6 5 4 3 2 1

CONTENTS

INTRODUCTION

What does it mean to have a heart of mercy?

Maybe you don't feel like you are a particularly merciful person. Maybe you desire to cultivate a heart of mercy but aren't sure how. Maybe you've been told you have a gift of mercy but would like to be more intentional about using that gift for God's glory.

I remember years ago when I went on my first mission trip to Haiti. Before the trip, our leader had us take a spiritual gifts test. We spent time as a group talking through each person's top three spiritual gifts and how they might be useful on the trip and with our team.

One of my top three gifts was mercy. Honestly, I didn't really know what that meant. I had a hunch it had something to do with compassion and love, but I was curious to learn more.

That first trip to Haiti helped me begin to understand that God has a heart of mercy. He cares deeply for the widow, the orphan, the single mom, and the immigrant. The plight of these people weighs heavy on my heart too, but sometimes I'm not exactly sure what to do with these feelings. Just how does God want me to extend mercy to others?

This Bible study is designed to meet you in your questions about mercy. You don't have to travel to another country to understand God's heart for mercy or to demonstrate it to others. We will consider our own desperate need for mercy, how we must first receive it before we are then called to extend mercy to others in our everyday lives and beyond.

For the next six weeks, we're going on a treasure hunt through Scripture to learn more about how to cultivate a heart of mercy. We will study the stories of Old and New Testament characters who were granted mercy and who multiplied mercy to others. Our prayer is that this study will encourage you to learn more about God and yourself. Friend, we are journeying alongside you!

How to Use This Study

Create in Me a Heart of Mercy is designed to be used by individuals or small groups. For groups doing this study, we recommend allowing at least forty-five minutes for discussion (or more for larger groups).

As you're working through this study, we encourage you to take your time and go at your own pace. We believe God has an incredible message for each one of us in His Word, and we will find it when we seek to learn more and go deeper into Scripture. We pray this study can be an encouraging, life-giving experience that brings you closer to God rather than being just one more thing on your to-do list. Ask God to reveal His insight and truth to you. Then listen as He speaks to you through His Word.

> Enhance your community study experience with our *Create in Me a Heart of Mercy* leader guide. Go to incourage.me/leaderguides to download your free small group resources.

Each week of this study will begin with a personal story from an (in)courage contributor on day 1, following our habit of "going first" with our hard, messy, real stories. Many of these stories begin in deep heartache but inevitably find their way back to God and the great gift of mercy He's given us. We will also provide a memory verse to work on throughout each week that will help root the concepts of mercy in the soil of your heart.

The other four days we will dive deep into God's Word to discover the source of mercy in our lives, how mercy transformed the lives of different people in the Bible, and the impact mercy can have on our lives today.

Are you ready? We at (in)courage are so thrilled to go on this journey with you! Join us as we ask God to create in us hearts of mercy.

WHAT IS MERCY?

When you think of the word *mercy*, what comes to mind?

Maybe you think about someone raising their hands and pleading, "Mercy!" like a white flag of surrender.

Maybe you think of a person offering forgiveness to someone who has deeply hurt them.

Maybe you think of a child begging for food on the streets, and it pricks something deep inside you.

As we begin this study, we'll be looking at three key biblical definitions of mercy and the dynamic ways God exemplifies mercy for all of us. *Easton's Bible Dictionary* defines *mercy* as simply "compassion for the miserable."[1] This week we will be exploring early examples of God's mercy in the lives of Adam and Eve as well as Sarah, Abraham, and Hagar.

Biblical mercy is love reaching out to meet a need without considering the merit of the person who receives the aid.[2] However, the concept of mercy is much more layered and nuanced than we might think. It encompasses other words in the Bible like grace, pity, love, kindness, hospitality, forgiveness, and favor. The Hebrew word *hesed* is often used to describe God's abundant mercy and faithfulness toward His children. That includes us! We will explore that definition more deeply in week 3.

In today's story, Lucretia Berry tells how she experienced God's compassion and mercy through the divorce of her parents.

A Story of Mercy

You are disposable! The gravitational pull of that false message trapped nine-year-old me in its orbit when my parents divorced. In the breakup of their marriage, my mom was awarded primary custody of my brother and me, my dad was given significant visitation rights, and nine-year-old me inherited the false message that I didn't matter.

No one actually spoke those words to me. But the upheaval, grief, and wounding from that childhood trauma left me with scars. Like a skillful makeup artist, I learned to hide them. Achievements and accolades were the perfect concealer, and having a boyfriend meant that at least I mattered to someone, even if he didn't truly respect me.

But beneath the homecoming queen crown, the college graduate honors, and the multiple degrees, the fear of being insignificant clung to me. It melded into me. It stayed with me and became seemingly inseparable. It speaks to who I am as a wife, as a mom:

You are disposable! You don't matter!

That fear wants to be my forever song, the score to my life's unfolding. It wants to be the lead vocal, and whenever I experience rejection, it turns up the volume and presses the Repeat button. It gets the spotlight and summons all my attention. Having this fear reverberating in the recesses of my being is exhausting. I lose sleep and agonize over the pain of feeling invisible and invaluable. It's a constant noise, and at times it's deafening:

You are disposable! You don't matter! You are insignificant!

I know God sees me and values me—that's not something I struggle with. My strife is with other people devaluing me. I feel deflated when people treat me like I don't matter. I can tell myself that what others think of me isn't important, that I should only be concerned with how God sees me and knows me. But that doesn't negate the countless times when I've been overlooked or felt like an afterthought or a pawn in someone else's decision-making process.

One particular time the anxiety pushed me to desperation, and I cried out to *El Roi*—"the God who sees." God is the one who not only sees me but sees everything. Through Hagar's story in Genesis 16, I know that God faithfully holds me when it seems as though I've been abandoned. And in moments like these, I feel like I shouldn't need God to affirm me, that mature faith doesn't need to be coddled. But desperation overrode my ego, and I recalled how Hagar received God's mercy. In my exhaustion, I became like a toddler who crawls into a nurturing lap to be embraced by mercy-filled arms.

As I surrendered, my life's major events unfolded in my mind like a movie recap. But in this re-viewing, I heard a different soundtrack— one resonating the mercy of El Roi. I began to clearly see elements at work that I had not given much attention to before. I grabbed my journal and started writing.

Who saw me when I thought I was invisible?

- During my parents' divorce, my grandma Pearline made sure I knew I was special to her.
- When my mom remarried and it seemed as though her new husband wanted her without her children, my grandma Virginia acknowledged my loneliness and pain.
- When I needed support along my academic journey, several people played key roles in escorting me from being a first-generation college student to becoming a college professor. It was a series of miracles.
- When I was in situations where someone was taking advantage of me, my husband intervened and shut down the whole operation.

Names and events flowed like a waterfall. I journaled for pages. The list went on and on of how mercy manifested through people seeing me, hearing me, and valuing me. As I reflected and recorded in my journal, the volume on the old song, which does not bear repeating, began fading into the background. I was ready to sing a new song:

I matter. I am seen. I am valued. I am heard.

When you feel vulnerable, invisible, or forgotten, remember that El Roi not only sees you but comes alongside you and cares for you.

In Matthew 6:26, Jesus reminds us, "Look at the birds of the air; they do not sow or reap or store away in barns, and yet your heavenly Father feeds them. Are you not much more valuable than they?" (NIV).

When lies try to deplete you, ask El Roi, the one who sees you, to remind you of your visibility, your value, and your significance. In His mercy, He will bring you back to truth. You matter. You are seen. You are valued. You are heard. Rehearse truth's song. Turn up the volume and allow it to refresh you.

—LUCRETIA BERRY

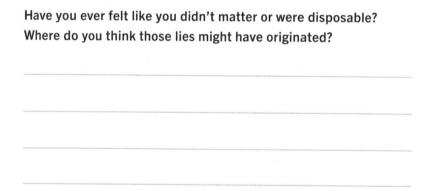

Have you ever felt like you didn't matter or were disposable? Where do you think those lies might have originated?

This week we will be exploring the stories of biblical characters who experienced God's mercy and presence in unexpected ways. It's important for us to understand how mercy has been part of God's plan from the very beginning.

Let's start by looking back in Scripture at God's first act of mercy toward Adam and Eve in Genesis 3, which we usually refer to as "the fall." This story will help us build a foundation for what mercy is and how God offers it to all humankind.

Read Genesis 2:15–17. What did God tell Adam about the tree of the knowledge of good and evil? What were the consequences if Adam did not obey God?

_____

_____

_____

_____

Read Genesis 3:1–19. How would you describe God's mercy in this story?

_____

_____

_____

_____

Adam and Eve experienced God's mercy in a personal way. We often focus on the consequences they faced for their disobedience rather than the profound act of mercy God offered them in this moment. God is setting a precedent for the future when He will send His Son, Jesus, as the ultimate act of mercy.

SCRIPTURE MEMORY MOMENT

This week's Scripture is Ephesians 2:4–5. Write the verses in your journal from the NIV as printed below or from your favorite translation. Throughout the week, commit these words to memory as you ask God to create in you a heart of mercy.

But because of his great love for us, God, who is rich in mercy, made us alive with Christ even when we were dead in transgressions—it is by grace you have been saved.

A PRAYER FOR TODAY

GOD, *thank You for having mercy on Adam and Eve and all of us. In these next several weeks, help me grow in my understanding of mercy. Thank You for seeing me in the midst of my own challenging circumstances like You saw Lucretia. I am reminded that because of You, I am never alone. I am deeply grateful for the way You redeem all things. Amen.*

But Abram said to Sarai, "Behold, your servant is in your power; do to her as you please." Then Sarai dealt harshly with her, and she fled from her.

The angel of the LORD found her by a spring of water in the wilderness, the spring on the way to Shur. And he said, "Hagar, servant of Sarai, where have you come from and where are you going?" She said, "I am fleeing from my mistress Sarai." The angel of the LORD said to her, "Return to your mistress and submit to her." The angel of the LORD also said to her, "I will surely multiply your offspring so that they cannot be numbered for multitude."

Genesis 16:6–10

Have you had a time when you were feeling miserable and in deep need of compassion? Describe that experience and how compassion was shown to you. If you were not shown compassion, how did that make you feel?

Sarai was Abram's wife, and at age sixty-five—about the time many of us retire—she joined her husband as they left their homeland and followed God's leading to the land of Canaan. Sarai had been childless her whole life, but in Genesis 12 and 15, God promises that Abram's offspring will outnumber the stars and that He will make a great nation through Abram's family.

Fast-forward ten years, and Sarai has grown impatient waiting for God's promise to be fulfilled. Sarai and Abram are now well into their seventies and eighties—far beyond the age of childbearing by human standards. So Sarai takes matters into her own hands and tells her husband to have sex with her servant Hagar so they can have children through her.

Although fathering children by servants or with multiple wives was culturally acceptable at that time, it was not God's plan for this chosen couple. Hagar was an Egyptian who likely had been given to Abram by Pharaoh back in Genesis 12 to serve as Sarai's maid. This young woman of color has no agency in this situation. She is sexually exploited, and when she becomes pregnant, Sarai physically abuses her. Hagar flees to the wilderness, which feels like a better option than staying in an abusive situation. Hagar is an outcast, wandering in the desert alone.

Take some time to read Genesis 16:1–15, which describes the angel of the Lord meeting Hagar in the wilderness. Some scholars say the Hebrew phrase translated as "the angel of the LORD" was used to indicate meeting with God Himself or perhaps that it's a reference to the preincarnate Christ.[3]

God seeks out Hagar in her misery and asks her two key questions: "Where have you come from and where are you going?" (Gen. 16:8). This is significant because God already knew where she came from and where she was going. He is the all-knowing God of the universe, yet He takes the time to ask her these two personal questions and gives her the opportunity to share her story. He sees her in her misery and gives her a chance to pour out her feelings. God tenderly leans in to engage with her.

Such tenderness would have been foreign to Hagar. She had experienced prejudice, injustice, and abuse throughout her life. Sarai and

Abram do not even call her by name—but God does! There is no greater mercy than to be seen by God Himself.

Brain science shows that telling our trauma stories is incredibly beneficial. Feelings of shame subside, unhelpful beliefs about the event are corrected, and the memory becomes less triggering.[4] Of course, we know that true healing comes from God, who invites each of us, as He invited Hagar, to tell our stories.

Not only does God care about Hagar's story but He also offers her a promise as a sign of His mercy and compassion.

Read Genesis 16:7–15 again. What does God promise Hagar, and why do you think it is significant?

_____

_____

_____

_____

Hagar responds to this promise by ascribing to God a name that honors the way she feels seen by Him: *El Roi*, "the God who sees." Hagar becomes the first person in the Old Testament to ascribe a name to God. Let that sink in. She names Him *El Roi*, "the God who sees."

Hagar also names a well or spring in the place where she met God, calling it *Beer-lahai-roi*, meaning "a well of the Living One who sees

When God sent His Son to earth as a human child, it was a profound act of mercy. He sent Immanuel to be *with us* as a physical presence here on earth.

me." The imagery here illustrates the way God refreshed and ministered to Hagar like a spring in the wilderness.

Similar comparisons are used in many places throughout the Bible. Psalm 23:2 talks about how God leads us beside quiet waters to restore us. Jesus meets the Samaritan woman at the well in John 4 and offers her "living water."

> **Being close to water is somehow both physically and spiritually refreshing. Have you ever hiked to a waterfall or spent the day on a river or lake? How did that place refresh you? Describe what it was like.**

> **Read Isaiah 43:16–21, which is a prophecy to the nation of Judah living in Jerusalem before the Babylonian conquest about God's mercy. As you read through these verses, what similarities do you see to the language in Genesis 16?**

In this passage from Isaiah, God's mercy is marked by something unexpected: a well in the desert. In the same way, God's mercy toward Hagar was unexpected. When she fled from Abram and Sarai, Hagar was miserable. After meeting with God, she possesses a new sense of courage. She fled to the desert in a state of utter despair but returns to Abram and Sarai's tent as a new woman known and loved by God. She carries with her the promise God gifted her, and when she later gives birth to her son, Abram names him Ishmael, which means "God hears."

Has God ever done anything unexpected in your life that you might call an example of His mercy? How did that make you feel?

SCRIPTURE MEMORY MOMENT

Write out Ephesians 2:4–5 on a sticky note or index card and hang it somewhere you will see it often. You might post it on your bathroom mirror, your car dashboard, or the refrigerator door so you can read it throughout the week and remind yourself that our God is "rich in mercy."

A PRAYER FOR TODAY

DEAR JESUS, *please help me hold on to Your promises even when I feel discouraged or in despair. You are like a well in the wilderness—a source of comfort and compassion—for me today. Thank You for the unexpected ways You have shown me mercy. Give me courage to navigate whatever trail You have me on today. Amen.*

DAY 3

The LORD passed before him and proclaimed, "The LORD, the LORD, a God merciful and gracious, slow to anger, and abounding in steadfast love and faithfulness, keeping steadfast love for thousands, forgiving iniquity and transgression and sin, but who will by no means clear the guilty, visiting the iniquity of the fathers on the children and the children's children, to the third and the fourth generation."

Exodus 34:6–7

Who has shown you mercy in the past? What were some of the person's actions toward you or words spoken to you that revealed their gift of mercy?

_____

_____

_____

_____

Many key events led up to the conversation between God and Moses in Exodus 34. God had shown His faithfulness and steadfast love for the people of Israel over and over again. In Exodus 14, God rescued the Israelites from slavery in Egypt and helped them cross the Red Sea. In Exodus 16, God provided manna from heaven and quail for them to eat in the wilderness. In Exodus 17, as they journeyed through the wilderness, the people cried out for water, and God commanded Moses to strike a rock that poured out water. In Exodus 20, God gave them the Ten Commandments as loving instructions on how to live during chaotic times. Later, in Exodus 32, as Moses returned after meeting with God on Mount Sinai, he caught the impatient people worshiping a golden calf idol. Angry and frustrated, Moses broke the two stone tablets of the Ten Commandments.

At his wits' end, in Exodus 34 Moses again ascends Mount Sinai to meet with God. There God appears to Moses in a cloud and proclaims who He is.

> Read Exodus 34:1–9. What particular character qualities of God are named in verses 6–7? How do you think these are related to mercy?

Theologian Tony Evans writes, "The Lord's words here tell us that God's love is not permissive. He is righteous and can overlook sin. That is, in fact, what makes the gospel such good news. In the cross of Christ, God's justice and God's love met."[5] We will be unpacking the intersection of justice and mercy in week 5, but it's important to acknowledge here that God is both just and merciful.

> Read Exodus 33:19 in the English Standard Version. What do you think the phrase "I . . . will show mercy on whom I will show mercy" means?

> The volume on the old song began fading into the background. I was ready to sing a new song: I matter. I am seen. I am valued. I am heard.
>
> —LUCRETIA BERRY

The apostle Paul quotes this verse in Romans 9 as he answers hypothetical objections that God has acted unjustly:

> What should we say then? Is there injustice with God? Absolutely not! For he tells Moses, I will show mercy to whom I will show mercy, and I will have compassion on whom I will have compassion. So then, it does not depend on human will or effort but on God who shows mercy. (vv. 14–16 CSB)

Paul emphasizes that to act unjustly would be outside of God's character. Showing mercy doesn't contradict that. Rather, God's mercy demonstrates that He is a good and caring Father.

Just a chapter earlier, Paul reminds us that we are adopted children of God. "But you have received the Spirit of adoption as sons, by whom we cry, 'Abba! Father!' The Spirit himself bears witness with our spirit that we are children of God" (Rom. 8:15–16).

What is your relationship like with your father? Has he been an example of mercy to you? Does that make it harder or easier to think about God as the Father of mercy?

When I was a child, I didn't see my father express a lot of emotion unless he was angry. He would praise me on the soccer field or if I got good grades, but he didn't always tell me he loved me or shower me with affection. I still remember the day my dad drove me to college for my freshman year. I was filled with excitement and nervousness as I anticipated moving away from home.

As we were driving, I looked over at my dad and saw tears streaming down his face. I was stunned because I had only seen my dad cry maybe once or twice in my eighteen years of life. Although he was very supportive of my attending college, he was overcome with emotion that day at the thought that I was moving away. I realized in that moment the depth of my dad's love for me. His tears expressed far more than words ever could and gave me a deeper love and gratitude for my daddy.

Whether or not we have a good relationship with our earthly father, we are invited to connect with God as the Father of mercy. As we saw on day 1 through Lucretia's story and on day 2 through Hagar's story, God shows Himself to be a compassionate Father over and over again. He doesn't always give us what we want or wish for, but He offers us His very presence, which is a gift of mercy.

Read Psalm 84 in the translation of your choice. Pay particular attention to verse 11. How does this psalm speak to you about God being a good and merciful Father?

SCRIPTURE MEMORY MOMENT

Read Ephesians 2:4–5 two or three times. See if you can start memorizing the first few phrases of the passage. Say them out loud to yourself or a family member for accountability.

A PRAYER FOR TODAY

DEAR LORD, *I am grateful for Your grace, patience, steadfast love, and faithfulness. No matter what my relationship looks like with my earthly father, thank You for being a perfect example to me of a father's love. Help me to be like You and to show compassion and mercy to others around me. Amen.*

And as for Ishmael, I have heard you: I will surely bless him; I will make him fruitful and will greatly increase his numbers. He will be the father of twelve rulers, and I will make him into a great nation.

Genesis 17:20 NIV

What does the word *blessing* mean to you? What comes to mind when someone says they are "blessed"?

_____

_____

_____

_____

Blessed is a word we throw around a lot in our culture. T-shirts, Christmas cards, and wall hangings proclaim phrases like "Thankful. Grateful. Blessed." Some people use #blessed as a popular hashtag on social media. But what does *blessed* really mean? Is it more than material wealth and happy family photos?

In the biblical context, the word *blessed* often refers to God's favor, strength, and ability to make His people fruitful. Blessing is not something that is earned but that is given freely by God and often in unexpected ways.

Sound familiar? Yes, blessing is an expression of God's mercy. God did not owe anything to Hagar and her son. In fact, He had chosen to make a covenant with Abram and Sarai's family and had promised that their descendants would outnumber the stars (Gen. 15:5). Yet, in His mercy, God also bestowed blessing on Hagar's son, Ishmael.

On day 2, we read about Hagar's predicament and how God saw her in the desert. God told Hagar to return to Abram's household where she would give birth to a son. According to Genesis 16:15–16, Abram was eighty-six years old when Ishmael was born.

> **What does God tell Abram in Genesis 17:20–21? Why do you think this is significant?**

God's covenant blessings are reserved for Sarai's son, Isaac, but blessings are also promised to Hagar's son, Ishmael. This is the multiplication of God's mercy in Hagar's life. God's generosity is on display for all to see through Hagar and Ishmael's story.

> **Do you have any experiences where someone has been unexpectedly generous toward you? Describe what they did for you and how it made a difference for you.**

When I was in my early twenties, I had accrued a large amount of credit card debt. I was a single girl floundering in a new city and a new job. My engagement had recently ended, and I felt like I was in a deep pit with no shovel to dig myself out.

Some dear friends of mine from college, whom I'd kept in close contact with, reached out one day. They said they wanted to help me by paying off my credit card debt and setting me up with a financial planner to walk me through making some goals for the future. I was floored by their offer! Such generosity was unexpected and humbling. They had no expectations that I would pay them back. Instead, they were simply motivated by love and compassion for my situation.

This gift changed the trajectory of my life in many ways. Those friends helped me dig myself out of a pit that seemed to keep getting deeper and darker. They also set me on a path with some new tools to avoid similar pits in the future.

I didn't deserve to have someone bail me out in that situation, but my friends' compassion was an act of mercy. I'm deeply grateful for this generosity that decades later still shapes the way I handle money. This is an example of generous mercy.

> **Write out Psalm 24:1. This verse serves as a reminder that God owns everything. How does this truth shape your perspective about generosity?**

If God owns everything, then we are designed to operate as stewards of the resources He gives us. When we are able to see God as the owner and ourselves as property managers of His resources—time, money, skills—we are able to pivot away from pride and entitlement and toward generosity that serves God and others.

The Bible includes a lot of instructions about money and possessions. In fact, sixteen of Jesus's thirty-eight recorded parables center on this theme. This is a strong indication that Jesus cared about the way we perceive and deal with money and riches. In addition, Paul writes instructions about wealth in several of his letters, including his letter to Timothy, who was ministering in Ephesus. That city was a thriving commercial and religious center strategically located on the major east–west trade route near the southern coast of Asia Minor.

> Read 1 Timothy 6:17–18. Paul turns the idea of riches and wealth on its head. These verses remind us not to be prideful about our prosperity and to be rich in generosity. How do you imagine this would be different from the way people in Timothy's context (or even in our present-day context) typically measured riches and wealth?

SCRIPTURE MEMORY MOMENT

Take time today to recite Ephesians 2:4–5. As you do, reflect on ways you can show mercy through generosity this week.

A PRAYER FOR TODAY

DEAR GOD, *thank You for extending merciful generosity toward all of us. You provide for us in such creative ways. Help me turn away from feelings of pride and entitlement in regard to material riches. Open my eyes and heart to ways that You might want me to extend mercy and generosity to those around me this week. Amen.*

DAY 5

But Sarah saw the son of Hagar the Egyptian, whom she had borne to Abraham, laughing. So she said to Abraham, "Cast out this slave woman with her son, for the son of this slave woman shall not be heir with my son Isaac." And the thing was very displeasing to Abraham on account of his son. But God said to Abraham, "Be not displeased because of the boy and because of your slave woman. Whatever Sarah says to you, do as she tells you, for through Isaac shall your offspring be named. And I will make a nation of the son of the slave woman also, because he is your offspring." So Abraham rose early in the morning and took bread and a skin of water and gave it to Hagar, putting it on her shoulder, along with the child, and sent her away. And she departed and wandered in the wilderness of Beersheba.

Genesis 21:9–15

Have you ever experienced an extreme reaction from someone you offended? If not, have you witnessed a situation in which a person's reaction seemed like a harsher response than the original offense warranted?

In Genesis 21, something in Sarah snaps. This would not have been the first time Ishmael and Isaac interacted as brothers. As the passage indicates, Ishmael was laughing at his baby brother. Several translations say he was not just laughing but actually mocking him. Sarah is deeply offended by Ishmael's laughter and goes to the extreme of urging Abraham to send Hagar and Ishmael away.

The irony is that the name Isaac is derived from the Hebrew verb *tsahaq*, which means "he laughs." A Hebrew audience would have understood this play on words. Ishmael was caught laughing at his brother named Laughter. The scene proves even more ironic when we recall that back in Genesis 18:12, Sarah was caught laughing to herself at the thought of birthing a child in her old age.

> **Reread Genesis 21:10. What is the real reason Sarah wants Abraham to send Ishmael and Hagar away? How does this influence her reaction?**

In ancient Near Eastern culture and even in Middle Eastern culture today, family inheritance is very important. In Abraham and Sarah's time, the firstborn son would always receive a larger inheritance and a place of honor in the family. Even if the first son was birthed by a surrogate wife, that mother and child were not allowed to be sent away, even if the man's first wife later bore a son.[6]

This was certainly on Sarah's mind. She does not want Isaac forced to share his inheritance with his brother. We can also infer that she doesn't want to have to share a household with Hagar for the rest of her life. Although it grieves Abraham, God tells him to listen to Sarah and send Hagar and Ishmael away.

> **Read Genesis 21:14–21. How does God show mercy to Hagar and Ishmael in this passage?**

> **Can you recall what Ishmael's name means? (Hint: Reread Gen. 16:11.) What are some examples from your own life when God heard your cries for help and mercy?**

Again, God's mercy toward Hagar and Ishmael is paramount in this scene. They clearly experience much suffering in being sent away, but *God hears* Hagar's cries and the voice of Ishmael. God provides for their physical needs by showing Hagar a well of water. And we learn that God provides for Ishmael throughout his lifetime: "God was with the boy, and he grew; he settled in the wilderness and became an archer. He settled in the Wilderness of Paran, and his mother got a wife for him from the land of Egypt" (Gen. 21:20–21 CSB).

What a powerful and promising statement! Ishmael's life is never easy-peasy or #blessed, but through it all God is *with* him. If we follow Ishmael and his family through history, we discover that God makes good on His promise to make a great nation through Ishmael's offspring as well as through Isaac's.

> **Read Isaiah 7:14 and Matthew 1:23. What is the name given to the child prophesied in these verses, and what does that name mean?**

_____

_____

_____

_____

Throughout the Old Testament, God was *with* His chosen people. He was *with* Abraham, Sarah, and Isaac. He was *with* vulnerable people like Hagar and Ishmael. All of this was preparation for His bigger plan to send mercy in the form of a person. When God sent His Son to earth as a human child, it was a profound act of mercy. He sent Immanuel to be *with us* as a physical presence here on earth. We will unpack this more in week 2 as we examine why we need mercy and also in week 3 when we discuss how we receive mercy.

God takes the time to ask Hagar these two personal questions and gives her the opportunity to share her story. He sees her in her misery and gives her a chance to pour out her feelings.

How have you experienced God as Immanuel, "God with us," through difficult circumstances?

_____

_____

_____

_____

SCRIPTURE MEMORY MOMENT

Share Ephesians 2:4–5 with a family member or friend. Reflect with that person on how these verses have become meaningful to you over this last week.

A PRAYER FOR TODAY

DEAR GOD, *please bring to mind anyone I need to forgive or to ask forgiveness from this week. Thank You for meeting me in the desert places when I feel betrayed or abandoned. I am grateful You hear me in my grief and suffering. You are my helper and my provider. Remind me this week that You are with me in all circumstances. Amen.*

WHY DO WE NEED MERCY?

In week 1 of this study, we looked at some definitions of mercy and unpacked the story of God's mercy to Hagar from Genesis 16. This week we're continuing down the path of understanding mercy by asking this foundational question: Why do we need mercy?

No one has a right to mercy. It is something that is freely given out of compassion and love. When we understand this, we gain a deeper appreciation of God's goodness and generosity toward us. We can then "with confidence draw near to the throne of grace, that we may receive mercy and find grace to help in time of need" (Heb. 4:16).

Mercy and grace are inextricably linked. Think about them as a dynamic duo that work together in God's kingdom. We can't understand grace without understanding God's mercy, and vice versa.

In Simi John's story below, we get to witness how both grace and mercy were extended to her in a life-threatening car accident. As you read Simi's story, consider how these two qualities are similar and different.

A Story of Mercy

They say you never forget your firsts. Well, I know I will never forget my first car wreck.

I was eighteen and carelessly talking on the phone while driving home at night in my mom's Lexus. I remember turning left and feeling a great impact that caused the car to spin multiple times. When it finally came to a stop, I looked up to see a dark red truck flipped on its side in front of me. I went into shock and gaped at my little brother in the passenger seat. I kept repeating, "I hit someone!"

Being the calmer one in that moment, my brother asked for my cell phone to call our dad. I refused to hand it over because I just knew my dad would be furious with me. We were an immigrant family, and for us this used Lexus was a symbol of the American Dream come true. My parents both worked full-time jobs and ran a catering business on the weekends to help provide for our family. I had ruined their prized possession.

My brother ripped the phone from my hand and called my dad. I saw something move by the truck. A man emerged carrying in his arms what looked like his daughter. I began to shake, wondering if she was alive or dead. My heart was beating out of my chest. The scene felt like a really bad dream. I saw him place her feet down on the ground, and she began to walk. I breathed a sigh of relief.

He walked up to my window, and I asked, "Are y'all okay?"

He looked into my eyes and said these words I will never forget: "Are we okay? You destroyed the only automobile I own!"

Tears began to flow down my face like a waterfall as his words sank into my soul. I had ruined his life.

Flashes of red and blue lights and loud sirens quickly overtook the scene on that dark, humid night. I sat on the median and wept at the thought that I almost killed another human being. I didn't want to face my dad, because I didn't know how I would explain the mess I had created. It was all my fault, and I couldn't fix any of it.

I felt helpless and sat there wishing I could go back in time. I saw my dad's car coming close and began to weep harder, burying my head between my knees. He was going to see the damage I had caused. He wasn't just going to be angry about the price he would have to pay to fix it, but he would be disappointed in me too. I sat on that median with the great weight of guilt and shame on my heart.

As I looked up, I saw my dad get out of his car and look around. Our eyes met. He ran toward me, scooped me up off that median, and patted me down. "Are you hurt?" he asked.

I shook my head and fell into his arms. He hugged me tight and told me to go sit in his car while he took care of everything. As I sat in the safety of my dad's car, away from the nightmare, I watched my dad walk up to the other driver and talk to the police officers on my behalf. The drive home was quiet.

My dad came to my room that night because nobody could really sleep, and he told me, "Accidents happen. We have insurance to take care of all the stuff, but the important thing is that everyone is safe." It made me feel a little better, but in the days that followed, I realized the effects of the accident. I became paralyzed with fear of getting behind the wheel again and eventually decided to give up driving altogether.

But my dad refused to let the wreck define me. He took the whole family to the Honda dealership to pick out a new car—a brand-new Civic. He asked me to pick the color because it was going to be my car. I was so confused. Why would my dad want to buy a brand-new car for me when I had just totaled their prized possession? It didn't seem to make any sense because I knew I didn't deserve it.

That was the moment I really understood the depth of mercy.

Though I became a Christian at age thirteen, I hadn't really grasped the meaning of mercy. And I was definitely not good at showing mercy to others when they failed. Instead, I was legalistic and judgmental. As the oldest child in my family, I was naturally a rule follower and a great student who never got in trouble. Growing up in an Indian home, in a shame-honor culture, it was important for me to do all the right things. I was good at being good. I knew how to check all the boxes and do what was required of me. But after that day, I finally began learning about something even more important than "being good."

Mercy is a mystery; it doesn't make sense. Mercy comes running in when we are in the middle of our mess and wraps us in a love we don't deserve and can't fully grasp. The night of my car wreck I saw love and forgiveness collide, and I was met with mercy.

—SIMI JOHN

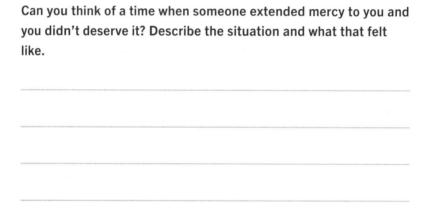

Can you think of a time when someone extended mercy to you and you didn't deserve it? Describe the situation and what that felt like.

Our heavenly Father gifts us mercy in much the same way Simi's father did. Her father was more concerned about his daughter's well-being than about punishing her for what she did wrong. The same is true of God. He loves us with generous mercy and offers up amazing grace.

In English Bible translations, the words *mercy* and *grace* are often coupled together in both the Old and New Testaments.[1] In the book of Psalms, David and the other writers speak frequently about God's grace and mercy. Psalm 103 is just one example of a praise psalm intended to glorify and honor God by proclaiming who He is.

Read Psalm 103:1–12. Write down the descriptions that talk about God's grace and mercy, which spring from His deep love for us.

_____

_____

_____

_____

What did you learn about God's mercy from these descriptions? Was anything especially meaningful or comforting to you?

_____

_____

_____

_____

According to this psalm, does God give us what we deserve? Explain.

_____

_____

_____

_____

In his book *Even If*, Pastor Mitchel Lee writes, "The life-transforming truth is that we are left not at the mercy of our situations but rather at the mercy of a loving God who leads us and does have wonderful plans for us."[2] He goes on to explain that when we remind ourselves who God is and what He has done for us, then we will develop a "reflex-like" disposition for our faith. Even if life situations are challenging, this disposition will help us trust God in ways we never thought possible and walk in peace and hope for the future. This is exactly what David is doing in Psalm 103.

SCRIPTURE MEMORY MOMENT

This week's memory verse is Psalm 23:6, which serves as a reminder to us of God's love and faithfulness to David and to us. Write the verse in your journal from the English Standard Version as printed here or from your favorite translation that includes the word *mercy*. Throughout the week, commit these words to memory as you meditate on what it means to have goodness and mercy follow you.

Surely goodness and mercy shall follow me
all the days of my life,
and I shall dwell in the house of the LORD
forever.

A PRAYER FOR TODAY

DEAR GOD, *I need Your grace and mercy even more than I realized. Thank You for redeeming my life and showing me compassion. Help me have a reflex-like disposition that trusts You at all times. Remind me that Your goodness and mercy are always with me. Create in me a heart of mercy that mirrors Yours. Amen.*

And the son said to him, "Father, I have sinned against heaven and before you. I am no longer worthy to be called your son." But the father said to his servants, "Bring quickly the best robe, and put it on him, and put a ring on his hand, and shoes on his feet. And bring the fattened calf and kill it, and let us eat and celebrate. For this my son was dead, and is alive again; he was lost, and is found." And they began to celebrate.

Luke 15:21–24

Have you ever pursued something you thought would be fun or rewarding but turned out to be disappointing or even harmful? What did you learn from that situation?

This week we are going to focus on the parable of the prodigal son. Let's lean in to see how mercy is displayed in this story. This parable is one of three recorded in Luke 15 that illustrate the deep love God has for wayward sinners. As Jesus was telling these stories, the tax collectors and sinners were approaching to listen. The Pharisees and scribes were there too, complaining about how Jesus welcomed sinners and ate with them. The audience is key to the story. Jesus was addressing a mixed group of Jews and gentiles, those who were considered righteous and those who were regarded as sinners. He has a word for all of them in this parable. And there's also a word for those of us reading it today.

> **Read Luke 15:11–24. Pay particular attention to how the younger son is transformed in this story. How does his attitude change from the beginning when he sets out to the end when he returns home?**

In this parable, the younger son wants to spread his wings and experience freedom, but in the process he squanders what his father gave him. He falls into such a horrible predicament that he finds himself feeding pigs, which are considered unclean animals by the Jews. And even the pigs are in a better situation than he is—at least they have something to eat! The son finally decides to return home and beg for mercy, but before he can even confess what he has done, his father embraces him with love and acceptance.

Mercy is a mystery; it doesn't make sense. Mercy comes running in when we are in the middle of our mess and wraps us in a love we don't deserve and can't fully grasp.

—SIMI JOHN

In the text, we read that the prodigal doesn't consider himself worthy to be called his father's son because of what he has done. "Make me like one of your hired servants," he says (Luke 15:19 NIV). The father's response is unexpected. Instead of scolding his son or chastising him for his irresponsible behavior, he runs to him and throws his arms around him and kisses him. He showers him with gifts, food, and a grand welcome-home party. The father offers his younger son the gift of mercy.

> **What are the gifts the father offers his son and why do you think these gifts were significant?**

The New Living Translation paints a vivid picture of what the father is saying: "'We must celebrate with a feast, for this son of mine was dead and has now returned to life. He was lost, but now he is found.' So the party began" (Luke 15:23–24). Can you imagine that party? This is a sign of lavish grace and forgiveness from the father. The younger son confesses his sins to his father and then accepts his father's gifts. The father and son are truly able to celebrate together because their relationship has been restored. It's one grand homecoming!

The reality is that all of us are born sinners who deserve consequences for our actions. Not a single one of us can live a completely sinless life. And even if we could, we still carry the stain of Adam's original sin. Romans 5:8 reminds us, "But God showed his great love for us by sending Christ to die for us while we were still sinners" (NLT). Jesus Christ embodies God's mercy.

Is it difficult for you to receive the Father's mercy and great love toward you? Why or why not?

Mary, the mother of Jesus, sang a song of praise to God the Father called the Magnificat. Her beautiful words, recorded in Luke 1:46–55, came in response to the greeting of her cousin Elizabeth, who called Mary blessed for carrying the Messiah in her womb. Mary's hymn speaks of the deliverance of Israel and tells of the grace that is to come for gentiles and Jews alike.

Read Luke 1:50. What does this verse from the Magnificat say about who will receive God's mercy?

When we fear God, we worship and revere Him in response to His mercy and faithfulness. Proverbs 1:7 from the Amplified Bible also helps illuminate what this "fear of the Lord" entails: "The [reverent] fear of the LORD [that is, worshiping Him and regarding Him as truly awesome] is the beginning and the preeminent part of knowledge [its starting point and its essence]; but arrogant fools despise [skillful and godly] wisdom and instruction and self-discipline."

The fear of the Lord enables us to truly receive His mercy, which we will talk about more next week.

SCRIPTURE MEMORY MOMENT

Write out Psalm 23:6 in your journal or on a notecard. How has God gifted you mercy? Now text this verse to a friend who might be encouraged by it today. Invite them to memorize it with you!

A PRAYER FOR TODAY

DEAR FATHER, *thank You for Your lavish mercy and grace. I confess my selfishness and sin to You today. Thank You for dying for me while I was still a sinner and for welcoming me home with open arms. Help me enter into true celebration with You and to savor Your mercy and grace. Amen.*

DAY 3

Meanwhile, the older son was in the fields working. When he returned home, he heard music and dancing in the house, and he asked one of the servants what was going on. "Your brother is back," he was told, "and your father has killed the fattened calf. We are celebrating because of his safe return."

Luke 15:25–27 NLT

Have you ever felt jealous of a blessing someone else received? How did you respond?

_____

_____

_____

_____

Read Luke 15:25–32. Can you relate to the older son's response in this section? Why or why not?

_____

_____

_____

_____

Jealousy is a powerful force that, if left unchecked, can consume our thoughts, bleed into our actions, and eventually poison our relationships. According to Jewish tradition, the oldest son in a family would be given a double portion of the inheritance. In a family with two sons, that meant the older son would receive two-thirds of the father's estate. Even so, the older son in this parable is overcome by jealousy. He can't stand that his brother, who misused their father's resources on wild living, would somehow be rewarded.

In Paul's first letter to the church of Corinth, he includes a description of what love looks like: "Love is patient and kind. Love is not jealous or boastful or proud or rude. It does not demand its own way. It is not irritable, and it keeps no record of being wronged" (1 Cor. 13:4–5 NLT). This is the opposite of how the older son in Jesus's parable acts toward his brother. The older son is blinded by his own sin of jealousy while keeping a tight tally of his brother's sins. Remember that this parable was told in the presence of the Pharisees and scribes, who were angry that Jesus was so welcoming toward tax collectors and sinners.

What message do you think Jesus was trying to convey to the religious leaders through this parable? What is a takeaway for you personally?

In Galatians 5:19–21, Paul lists the acts of the flesh that are contrary to the Spirit of God. What are these acts of the flesh? Why do you think jealousy is included?

I'm sure all of us have struggled with jealousy from time to time. We live in a culture that sets us up for constant comparison. Comparison is a tool Satan uses to divide, discourage, and isolate us, and it keeps us from flourishing together in community. Just think about all the Bible stories that deal with jealousy and envy: Cain and Abel, Jacob and Esau, Rachel and Leah—even Jesus's disciples had to work through the jealousy and envy among them.

Friendships grow toxic, neighbors keep to themselves, and marriages grow bitter because of envy and jealousy. As a mama of three daughters, I'm realizing it's important to process these feelings regularly. I need to model for my daughters how to combat envy that creeps up on us even in the smallest ways. We need to call out jealousy and encourage each other to turn away from it.

The core dilemma is what to do with our feelings of jealousy and envy. Here are a few strategies:

Bounce jealous or envious thoughts. In other words, if I look at someone or see something that makes me feel jealous or envious, I bounce that thought out of my mind and don't let myself dwell on it. I turn away from the scarcity mindset that tells me there's not enough to go around.

Rejoice with that other person. I might send a quick word of encouragement, share a compliment, write a card, or simply whisper a word out loud to myself and rejoice with that person for the gift they've been given.

Pivot toward something edifying. If I notice I have consistent feelings of jealousy or envy showing up while scrolling social media or interacting online, I take a break and spend time in God's Word. I also may reach out to connect with my family or with another friend who helps me refocus.

Offer up gratitude. In a season when I was navigating grief and fighting back envy, I wrote out the gifts God gave me each day in a journal. I thanked Him for the swirling colors of the sunset, the sink full of dirty dishes, my two-year-old's contagious giggles, and the breath in my lungs. This practice has helped me reframe my days and shift my attitude.

Immediately following the list of "acts of the flesh" in Galatians 5, Paul lists the fruit of the Spirit: love, joy, peace, patience, kindness, goodness, faithfulness, gentleness, and self-control (vv. 22–23). These come through the Holy Spirit and provide refreshment to others. Let's pray for the Holy Spirit to help us pivot away from jealousy and fill us with the abundant fruit that comes from walking close to Him.

> **Read Luke 15:7 and 15:10, which conclude the other two parables Jesus told on this occasion. How do these verses further illuminate God's mercy and love for the lost?**

In the parable of the prodigal son, the father's heart reflects our heavenly Father's heart that the lost will be found. In Luke 15:32, the father declares, "We had to celebrate this happy day. For your brother was dead and has come back to life! He was lost, but now he is found!" (NLT). We sense the father's exuberance in these words. Whether we relate more to the prodigal or to the older son—He is welcoming *all* of us home.

SCRIPTURE MEMORY MOMENT

Read Psalm 23:6 two or three times. Can you make it into a song? We are much more likely to memorize something that is set to music. You may already know a song that incorporates these lines, or feel free to make up your own!

A PRAYER FOR TODAY

DEAR JESUS, *I confess I'm letting jealousy and envy take over too many of my thoughts. Help me surrender these feelings back to You when they pop up. When I feel insecure, remind me who I am in Your eyes. Show me opportunities to collaborate and build others up. I'm deeply grateful that You welcome me home no matter what state I'm in. Amen.*

But he was angry and refused to go in. His father came out and en-
treated him, but he answered his father, "Look, these many years
I have served you, and I never disobeyed your command, yet you
never gave me a young goat, that I might celebrate with my friends.
But when this son of yours came, who has devoured your property
with prostitutes, you killed the fattened calf for him!" And he said
to him, "Son, you are always with me, and all that is mine is yours. It
was fitting to celebrate and be glad, for this your brother was dead,
and is alive; he was lost, and is found."

Luke 15:28–32

What do you believe gives you value or worth as a person?

The older son in Jesus's parable based his worth on merit. The concept
of merit involves being particularly good or worthy, especially to earn
praise or reward. You do something good or commendable and receive
a reward in return. Simi talked about this in her story back on day 1,
where she said it was important for her to do all the right things.

God expresses His extravagant love toward us through the sacrifice of His Son, Jesus. He calls us to a place of abundance rather than striving and scarcity.

Implicit in the idea of merit is entitlement. It's dangerous when we engage in relationships with a sense of entitlement, believing that people owe us something. In psychology such a relationship is referred to as *transactional* because its foundation is the expectation for reciprocation. Both people in the relationship are concerned with how the relationship might benefit them. The focus is on how much each person can get from the relationship instead of how much they can give. There is minimal consideration of the other person or willingness to sacrifice. Bonds are broken when one person doesn't perform, which makes these relationships constantly uncertain.[3]

We must be careful not to engage in our relationship with God this way. This would be treating God like a vending machine. We feed coins into a slot and in return we expect to get the candy bar we selected with the nuts and caramel. Similarly, we may pray or do something "religious" and expect God to deliver what we want in exchange.

Instead, God invites us into a relationship built on sacrifice. He expresses His extravagant love toward us through the sacrifice of His Son, Jesus. He calls us to a place of abundance rather than striving and scarcity.

Read Luke 15:28–30 again. Where do you see evidence of the older son's attitude of entitlement? What does he say that gives us a clue that he lives more by the concept of merit than mercy?

Pastor David Platt helps us understand how mercy and merit work in God's economy. He says, "Salvation is a free gift of divine mercy totally devoid of human merit."[4]

Read that quote again and let it sink in.

Salvation is totally free and not contingent on our human achievements or actions in any way. As Platt explains, mercy is free for us but costly for God, who sent His Son, Jesus, to earth to be murdered. This was part of God's plan. Jesus died as a substitute for the death we deserve. He took our place so that justice was served for our sins. When God offers us salvation, it is an act of outrageous mercy. His mercy is the forgiveness of our sins.

No other religion is based on this kind of mercy. Mercy is the crux of Christianity. We don't need to check off good behavior lists, prove ourselves through religious achievements, or earn our way like Simi wrote about in her story. Every other world religion is based on a system of merit.

Can you think of a time when someone offered you something of great value for free? How did that feel?

Read 2 Corinthians 3:17–18 in the English Standard Version. What do you think the word *freedom* means in this context?

We are gifted a free ticket to heaven if we simply choose to accept it from the Conductor. Anyone who chooses to believe and follow Christ steps onto a train of freedom from death and sin.

Let's think about what freedom means for Jewish believers. Their history included slavery in Egypt for 430 years. Every year at the celebration of Passover, they recount the story of how God emancipated them from slavery in Egypt and provided for them. Passover is a regular celebration of freedom.

In 2 Corinthians, Paul brings home this idea that life in Christ is freedom. This is especially meaningful coming from Paul because of his own history as a murderer of Christians. Paul was not some kind of Christian superhero; he needed grace as much as the rest of us.

Tara-Leigh Cobble writes, "Through God's power, Paul brings the ministry of life—which is far more glorious than the law, the ministry of death. The law can't solve sin, it can only name it. The ministry of death was glorious and necessary in its own right, but the ministry of life and grace far outshines it."[5] She helps us understand the contrast here between the law and grace. It's the difference between death and eternal life for those who believe.

> **Look up Galatians 5:1 (another of Paul's letters) in the New Living Translation and write it in the space below. (You can do this through BibleGateway.com or using a Bible app on your phone.) Why is it important to "stay free" and avoid getting caught up in the slavery of the law again?**

Consider your own life and name some areas where you find yourself getting caught up in the law or the rules instead of walking in the free gift of grace. For example, are you quick to judge others about their lifestyle, their politics, or even their lack of knowledge?

_____

_____

_____

_____

SCRIPTURE MEMORY MOMENT

Read Psalm 23:6 and visualize the details in this verse. Draw a little picture or write a description of what you think it might look like.

A PRAYER FOR TODAY

DEAR LORD, *I am so thankful for the sacrifice of Your Son, Jesus, who came as a substitute to die for my sins. Help me move away from any attitudes of entitlement in my life and relationships. Show me if there are ways I am getting caught up in the letter of the law instead of living in the freedom Christ died for. Amen.*

DAY 5

But you are a chosen race, a royal priesthood, a holy nation, a people
for his own possession, that you may proclaim the excellencies of
him who called you out of darkness into his marvelous light. Once
you were not a people, but now you are God's people; once you had
not received mercy, but now you have received mercy.

1 Peter 2:9–10

**Can you think of a time when you were chosen to do something
that made you feel either special or terrified?**

When I was in junior high and high school, my PE coaches would often
assign captains to pick teams when we were playing games like dodge-
ball and soccer. I discovered it was a privilege *and* a curse to be the
team captain because the captain was forced to make the hard choices.

Everyone in the class would line up nervously. The first captain would
pick a player. Then the second captain would pick a player. Then back
to the first captain. Choosing teammates required some strategy. A
captain might pick the most athletic girls first if she really wanted to

win the game. She might also consider choosing her friends first so she could hang out with them on the field.

I've always had a soft heart, so I would intentionally choose the kids I knew were going to get picked last. I hated the idea that someone would have to wait to be chosen until the very end. My heart was to show them grace and mercy, not just to build a team in the expected way.

Someone who is described as "chosen" is said to be the object of divine favor or is given a special privilege.[6] Throughout the pages of Scripture, this word *chosen* is used to mean elect, examined, preferred, and selected.

In the first two chapters of Genesis, we see God choose Adam and Eve as His special creation. Everything else God speaks into existence, but God chooses to bend low and form Adam from the dust of the earth. God also knew it was not good for Adam to be alone, so the Master Sculptor chooses to fashion Eve from one of Adam's ribs. Both the man and woman are created in the image and likeness of God according to Genesis 1:26.

Adam and Eve—and all of us—are chosen to be distinct spiritual and physical beings who reflect God's glory to the world. We have been given the privilege and task of stewarding creation well.

> **In light of this, read 1 Peter 2:9–10 from the English Standard Version. Peter is writing from Rome to the chosen believers who were "elect exiles" scattered throughout Asia Minor (see 1:1). Peter describes the believers in four different ways in verse 9. List these and take a guess at their significance to the recipients of his letter.**
>
> 1. _____
>
> 2. _____
>
> 3. _____
>
> 4. _____

Now read 1 Peter 2:9–10 in the vivid language of The Passion Translation as printed below. What do you imagine being "drenched" in mercy looks and feels like?

> But you are God's chosen treasure—priests who are kings, a spiritual "nation" set apart as God's devoted ones. He called you out of darkness to experience his marvelous light, and now he claims you as his very own. He did this so that you would broadcast his glorious wonders throughout the world. For at one time you were not God's people, but now you are. At one time you knew nothing of God's mercy, because you hadn't received it yet, but now you are drenched with it!

Can you think of a time when you were completely drenched? Maybe you were caught in a rainstorm or someone poured a bucket of water over you. Describe that memory and think of how it illustrates God drenching us in His mercy.

You are chosen to live in this era, this generation, this year with its many challenges and privileges. The story you are living today, the message you carry in your heart, the people you are leading and feeding—all of these present an opportunity to give God glory.

_____

_____

This passage also highlights our call as believers and recipients of God's mercy to "broadcast his glorious wonders throughout the world." There are many ways we can point others to His glory. Maybe it's telling a friend or someone we meet on an airplane about how God has transformed our lives. Maybe it's writing about God's glory in a book or posting photos on Instagram that show His glory. Maybe it's singing a song or composing a poem or painting a picture.

Friend, you are chosen. You are chosen to live in this era, this generation, this year with its many challenges and privileges. The story you are living today, the message you carry in your heart, the people you are leading and feeding—all of these present an opportunity to give God glory. Don't miss it!

> **Read Isaiah 43:10. Brainstorm a few ways that you might be a "witness" to God's glory for others. Think about your circles of influence, the people God has placed in your life, and the places you frequent. How can you creatively tell others about His mercy?**

_____

_____

_____

_____

SCRIPTURE MEMORY MOMENT

Review Psalm 23:6 one more time by saying it out loud. Then text it to a friend with a word of encouragement using something you've learned about mercy this week.

A PRAYER FOR TODAY

DEAR GOD, *thank You for drenching me in Your love and mercy today. I am humbled that You chose me to be Your witness in the world. Give me creativity and courage to share the story of Your glory with others in my spheres of influence. Amen.*

HOW DO
WE RECEIVE
MERCY?

Imagine someone gives you a giant gift for your birthday. The gift is wrapped in paper decorated with watercolor flowers and tied with a huge satin bow. You accept the gift from your friend with open hands, but then you put it in your office and never open it.

Wait . . . rewind. Would you do that?

I don't know about you, but I would be eager to open that gift. I would be so curious to see what's inside.

God gives us the miraculous gift of mercy. The heart of His mercy for us is salvation, which comes through His Son, Jesus, who died in our place. God meets us in our lack and our need for compassion. We're invited to respond to God's gift of mercy, not just hide it away in a room somewhere and wonder if we are worthy of it. The gift is free to us, as we talked about last week. But we must unwrap that package and discover the gift for ourselves.

Each of us also has unique, personal examples of God's gift of mercy in our lives. In this week's story, I'm sharing about when I became a widow and a suddenly single mom of three young girls at age thirty-seven. I needed God's mercy and compassion in that season of intense grief. Take note of how unwrapping His mercy changed everything for me.

A Story of Mercy

I still remember sitting at an outdoor café table across from my mama, who had been my spiritual mentor since I was a girl. In those days, when I was a newly minted widow, it was hard to find time away from my three young daughters to breathe and process. We savored our sandwiches on freshly baked bread and sipped cappuccino.

Our conversation wandered to the book of Ruth, which we were studying at our church. Was it any wonder that just a few months after my husband soared to heaven God would have me circle back to study one of my favorite books in the Bible that also happens to be about a young widow? The timing of it all was not lost on me.

I read through the book of Ruth with a new lens. The details of the story leaped off the pages of my Bible. What struck me most about Ruth's story was the way God extended mercy to her through others. She took a courageous step to follow Naomi's God, Yahweh, and this made all the difference for her future. Her situation turned from helpless to hopeful.

On that day at the café, my mama extended God's mercy to me. She looked into my eyes and said these words: "I want to encourage you to open your heart. I believe God has someone else for you."

My hands trembled. How could she suggest that God might bring a new man to our family when I was still in the depths of my grief? On some days the ache was still so heavy I felt like an actual boulder was sitting on my chest. It took all the strength I could muster to go to work and drive my kids to school.

My marriage with Ericlee had always anchored my life. The thought of dating someone new made me feel sick to my stomach. It was difficult to lift my head to imagine a new future, to imagine that God could redeem my situation. As far as I was concerned, my love story was dead and buried.

Lord, have mercy.

Even though my spirit was resistant, my mama planted seeds of hope in the soil of my heart that day, showing me God's mercy the way Naomi did for Ruth.

Another way God extended a hand of mercy to me was through my community. The grief journey is strange and unpredictable. I will forever be grateful for the dear friends who stepped onto the windy, uphill path of grief with me—including a man named Shawn.

I had met Shawn at the same time I met my late husband, Ericlee, on a mission trip to Haiti. Shawn and Ericlee were good friends from high school who shared many interests and passions. Shawn became my prayer partner on that trip and eventually was instrumental in bringing Ericlee and me together.

Shawn was a groomsman in our wedding and offered a toast at the reception. We traveled with Shawn. He visited us and celebrated the births of our three children with us. Through the years he supported our nonprofit in Haiti both prayerfully and financially.

Two years prior to Ericlee's death, Shawn was sitting in church and his pastor was preaching a series about God's heart for widows, orphans, refugees, and the poor. Something pricked Shawn's heart as he thought about his own mother, who was a widow living in California. Shawn lived in Maryland at the time but felt like God was calling him to move back home to help care for his mother. Ericlee and I prayed for Shawn as he looked for jobs in California, which was where we lived.

Ericlee was diagnosed with stage 4 cancer in May of the following year. The news hit us all like a sucker punch to the gut. Shawn came to visit that summer. We didn't realize that was the last time we would all be together. Ericlee graduated to heaven that September.

The week of Ericlee's funeral Shawn got a call from UCLA. They wanted to interview him for a position. It just so happened he already had tickets to travel through Los Angeles to the funeral and could do the interview in person. The following Monday they offered him the job. This wasn't a coincidence. In fact, this was just the beginning of how our sovereign God orchestrated every detail of Shawn's life to join with mine.

We kindled our relationship over many months. Shawn was the person who listened to me cry on the phone. He prayed over me. This was God's mercy—sending me a friend who loved Ericlee dearly and didn't put expectations on me through the grief journey.

Shawn drove from Los Angeles to Fresno to visit us on the weekends and spent quality time with the girls and me. Eventually, I began to look at him in a new way. My heart was opening, and those seeds of hope sprouted as God began to unfold His wild plan for our future. Despite my worries, our friends and families gave us their resounding blessing.

On our wedding day, our Author-God invited my three young daughters and me into a redeemed story only He could write. Out of our brokenness, God was bringing abundance.

More than seven hundred people filled the church to celebrate with us. These were the people who had prayed for Ericlee's healing and grieved with us. These were the people who stood by my side on my darkest days and lifted me up. That day in January was not just our wedding. It was a glory story our community wanted to be a part of because it spoke volumes about God's mercy and grace.

Shawn and I exchanged our vows under a painted red sign that proclaimed the word *glory* because we wanted everyone who attended our wedding to know that God was the one who deserved all the glory for bringing us together.

When I look back over our wedding pictures, joy and wonder still bubble up in my spirit. We laughed, we cried, we feasted, and we danced. God provided for all of us in a way we could not have imagined. He brought beauty from the ashes.

Friend, we serve a God of mercy. It's part of His character. Not every widow's story will turn out like mine. Not everyone will experience grief the same way my family has. But I know that the God of mercy is longing to meet you in your circumstances too. He was there for Ruth. And He was there for me.

I return to the words of David: "You have turned for me my mourning into dancing; you have loosed my sackcloth and clothed me with gladness, that my glory may sing your praise and not be silent. O LORD my God, I will give thanks to you forever!" (Ps. 30:11–12).

—DORINA LAZO GILMORE-YOUNG

Have you ever personally experienced God's provision or intervention during a time when you were vulnerable? What was that like?

_____

_____

_____

_____

Read Isaiah 61:1–3. Jot down the examples of God's mercy in this passage. Why are these significant?

_____

_____

_____

_____

This passage is the messianic prophecy that Jesus stands up to read in the synagogue in his hometown of Nazareth hundreds of years later (see Luke 4:18). Think about it like Jesus's job description. He came to fulfill these things. He came as a physical display of God's mercy.

God has given us a process for receiving His greatest gift of mercy—salvation. That process involves acknowledging and opening our hearts to His mercy, believing in His Son as our Savior, confessing our sins, and receiving forgiveness. If you haven't received that gift of mercy, I'd like you to consider it today. Talk to your leader, a pastor, or a friend about it if you have questions.

After we receive God's initial gift of mercy, we receive many other gifts of grace to open across a lifetime. God showed—and continues to show—His grace to me in my grief over my husband's death. Every day God shows me ways He is bringing beauty from our ashes.

This week we will be delving into the story of Ruth. This is not simply a love story with a predictable plot and a kiss at the end to seal the deal. Ruth is a book about God's providence in the midst of tragedy. Ruth is about dealing with disappointment, traversing grief, strengthening faith, and overcoming hardship. Ruth is about a courageous woman and a kind man who together exhibit the heart and character of God.

Ruth is a part of history—*His story*—the story of the Son of God who was sent to earth to be the ultimate redeemer for us all.

SCRIPTURE MEMORY MOMENT

This week's memory verse is Hebrews 4:16. The writer encourages believers to approach God boldly because of what He has done for them. Jesus can sympathize with us and intercede for us. In Him, we experience both mercy and grace in times when we are needy. Write the verse in your journal as printed below from the CSB or from your favorite translation. Throughout the week, commit these words to memory as you meditate on what it means to receive God's mercy.

Therefore, let us approach the throne of grace with boldness, so that we may receive mercy and find grace to help us in time of need.

A PRAYER FOR TODAY

DEAR LORD, *I am overwhelmed by Your mercy. Thank You again for this free gift You have offered to each one of us. I want to move toward You as I unwrap Your mercy and understand it in a deeper way. Help me receive it. Amen.*

DAY 2

But Naomi said to her two daughters-in-law, "Go, return each of you to her mother's house. May the Lord deal kindly with you, as you have dealt with the dead and with me. The Lord grant that you may find rest, each of you in the house of her husband!" Then she kissed them, and they lifted up their voices and wept.

Ruth 1:8–9

How has God met you in your grief? Can you think of a time when He gifted you His presence while you were grieving?

_____

_____

_____

_____

After Ericlee died, God was present with me in many ways and through many people. God also met me through the pages of the book of Ruth. Suddenly, Ruth was no longer a fairy tale to me. It was a living, breathing story that God was inviting me into. My heart felt the gravity of Ruth and Naomi's situation in a new way after I buried my beloved. I wept with Ruth and Naomi. Their sorrow was my sorrow. I understood the bond between them in a much greater way because of what I had endured. They learned to navigate grief together. God used His Word to show me His mercy and compassion.

Read Ruth 1:1–7. What do you learn about Ruth and Naomi's situation from this passage? Make a list of every detail that feels significant.

It's always important to consider the cultural context as we are reading the Bible. We learn from these verses that an Israelite man named Elimelech decided to leave his hometown of Bethlehem with his wife, Naomi, and their two sons. They headed to a country called Moab, which is east of the Dead Sea, while Jerusalem and Bethlehem are geographically west of the Dead Sea. The Moabites as a people group were descendants of an incestuous union between Lot and one of his daughters (see Gen. 19:30–38). They worshiped other gods and were hated by the Israelites.

There is no indication in the text that God sent Elimelech to Moab. We can assume he took his family there in search of food because of the famine in Israel, but we are not quite sure why Elimelech chose Moab.

While in Moab, Elimelech died. His sons had married Moabite women, even though God had specifically forbidden Israelites from intermarriage with the surrounding pagan nations. Mahlon married a girl named Ruth, and Chilion married Orpah. They all lived in Moab for ten years. During that decade, neither couple had any children, which in that culture was a deep disgrace and would have been a grief for their widowed mother, Naomi. Then Mahlon and Chilion also died, leaving their widowed wives and mother to fend for themselves.

Needless to say, these women were in a dire situation. The Hebrew word for widow is *almanah*, which comes from the root word *alem* meaning "unable to speak." This underscores the social rank of a widow in this ancient patriarchal culture. Without a father, husband, son, or other male relative to act in her defense, a widow had no voice and no rights. Widows were defenseless against abuse and exploitation and were considered among the most vulnerable members of society.[1]

In his book *Generous Justice*, Timothy Keller writes about God's heart for the "quartet of the vulnerable." God has special care and provision for these four groups of people: widows, orphans, immigrants, and the poor. His heart for these vulnerable groups is threaded all throughout the Bible.[2]

> **Read the following verses that help illuminate God's heart for vulnerable groups. What is the directive in these verses, and what does it reveal about God?**
>
> Deuteronomy 10:17–18
> Psalm 146:5–9
> Zechariah 7:9–10

Now, as we return to the book of Ruth, imagine it like the opening scene to a movie. The camera pans across the landscape to give us a view of Naomi and her two daughters-in-law on the dusty road leading back to Bethlehem. They are carrying all their belongings with them. The camera pulls in close to let viewers hear Naomi tell Ruth and Orpah, "Go back. Go home and live with your mothers. And may GOD treat you as graciously as you treated your deceased husbands and me. May GOD give each of you a new home and a new husband!" (Ruth 1:8 MSG).

The key words in Naomi's statement are "go back." In essence, these two words are releasing the two young widows from any obligation to take care of her, which was customary in their culture. The following verses tell us the women weep loudly together. Imagine this emotional moment on a large movie screen. The widows have endured much sorrow and loss in their ten years together. They cling to each other as their hearts are pulled in different directions.

When I imagine this scene, I can't help but think about my own grief journey and how it has bonded me to certain people. I'm deeply grateful for the friends who were physically and emotionally present for me during the early days of loss. My grief has also connected me with other young widows and with people who have lost loved ones in various ways.

Have you ever felt a bond with someone who experienced a loss similar to yours? How has grief connected you with others?

Read Ruth 1:8–18 in the translation of your choice. Take note of Naomi's words in verses 8–9. What is her desire for her daughters-in-law? How does this further show her care for them?

> The story you are living today, the message you carry in your heart, the people you are leading and feeding—all of these present an opportunity to give God glory.

In Ruth 1:8, Naomi says, "May the Lord *deal kindly* with you" (emphasis added). Different translations include some nuances in the phrasing: "may the LORD show kindness to you" (CSB); "may GOD treat you as graciously as" (MSG); "may the LORD deal faithfully with you" (CEB); "the Lord deal mercifully with you" (DRA).

The prominent word in these verses is the Hebrew word *hesed*. It's difficult to translate *hesed* into a single English word because it embodies a cornucopia of concepts, including mercy, loyalty, steadfast love, covenant faithfulness, and kindness. Bible scholar Carolyn Custis James explains, "*Hesed* is driven, not by duty or legal obligation, but by a bone-deep commitment—a loyal, selfless love that motivates a person to do voluntarily what no one has a right to expect or ask of them."[3]

The book of Ruth puts God's *hesed* on grand display. God's *hesed* blesses Naomi through the sacrifice and loyal commitment of her daughter-in-law Ruth. God's *hesed* also benefits Ruth as He showers her with both mercy and abundance through Boaz. And God's *hesed* raises up the loyal Boaz who grows in generosity and relationships.

Our memory verse from week 2 also employs that powerful word *hesed*: "Surely goodness and mercy [*hesed*] shall follow me all the days of my life, and I shall dwell in the house of the LORD forever" (Ps. 23:6). Now that we have a richer understanding of *hesed*, we have a fuller understanding of this verse. God's goodness, mercy, grace, kindness, and steadfast, loyal love follow us when we trust in Him.

SCRIPTURE MEMORY MOMENT

Copy Hebrews 4:16 onto an index card or sticky note. Put it in a place you will see it often, such as your car dashboard, the kitchen window above your sink, or your bathroom mirror. Be sure to read it throughout the week.

A PRAYER FOR TODAY

DEAR GOD, *thank You for meeting me in my grief and never leaving me alone. I'm grateful You provide encouragement through people and through Your Word. Help me learn more about the nuances of Your* hesed *and to receive it. Open my eyes to see those who are vulnerable in my circles of influence and who need a hand of grace and mercy. Amen.*

DAY 3

But Ruth replied, "Don't ask me to leave you and turn back. Wherever you go, I will go; wherever you live, I will live. Your people will be my people, and your God will be my God. Wherever you die, I will die, and there I will be buried. May the LORD punish me severely if I allow anything but death to separate us!" When Naomi saw that Ruth was determined to go with her, she said nothing more.

Ruth 1:16–18 NLT

Have you ever experienced the faithful devotion of a friend or family member in a hard season of life? Describe what it felt like to receive that.

_____

_____

_____

_____

Orpah finally obeyed Naomi's wishes that she return to her homeland, but Ruth was determined to stay with Naomi. These famous words from Ruth are often quoted at weddings as an expression of romantic love, but these powerful words actually are a statement of loyal love and commitment made by a daughter-in-law to her mother-in-law.

This passage serves as our first indication that Ruth is a courageous woman who is willing to follow her convictions—even standing up to her mother-in-law—to do what she feels is right. Ruth makes a radical decision to follow Naomi and Naomi's God—Yahweh. We see her risk-taking devotion in her response to Naomi in verses 16–18.

Author Carolyn Custis James describes Ruth this way: "Ruth stands out among all the biblical narratives as a powerful example of a person whose faith in God emboldens her with stunning courage. She gives us one of the strongest examples in all of Scripture of faith in action, and, as future scenes will show, a risk-it-all determination to live as a child of God."[4]

Has there been a time in your life when you had to make a hard decision to follow God? What was that experience like, and how did your faith grow during that time?

Ruth walks away from her home in Moab, her family of origin, her family's gods, and her past. Instead of walking down the aisle of a church to kneel at an altar and profess her faith, she walks down the dusty path to Bethlehem. She follows her empty-handed, brokenhearted mother-in-law in hopes of finding abundance. That act takes great humility and is key in acknowledging God's mercy and accepting His grace.

Read Proverbs 11:2 and James 4:6–10. What do you learn about humility from these verses?

We can imagine that Ruth had observed her mother-in-law's faith over the years they were together. She witnessed Naomi's faith through times of desolation and now humbly sacrifices to accept the uncertainties of lifelong widowhood in order to be faithful to Naomi and step into commitment to the one true God. This is a conversion moment for Ruth. On the road to Bethlehem, Ruth's life is transformed.

In Hebrew, the name *Bethlehem* means "house of bread." Again, this is no coincidence. Ruth might not have known it at the time, but trusting in God meant walking toward provision, healing, freedom, and eventually redemption for both her and Naomi.

> **Is there an area in your life where you want to see God bring healing and redemption today? What would it look like for you to humbly walk toward Bethlehem like Ruth did?**

If you've read or heard the Christmas story from Luke 2, you know that Jesus, God's Son, was born in Bethlehem. And in John 6, Jesus calls Himself the "bread of life."

> Truly, truly, I say to you, whoever believes has eternal life. I am the bread of life. Your fathers ate the manna in the wilderness, and they died. This is the bread that comes down from heaven, so that one may eat of it and not die. I am the living bread that came down from heaven. If anyone eats of this bread, he will live forever. And the bread that I will give for the life of the world is my flesh. (vv. 47–51)

Jesus, the bread of life, was born in Bethlehem, the house of bread. Bethlehem, then, is a symbolic place of provision, new life, redemption, and resurrection. Though Jesus would not be born for hundreds of years, Ruth and Naomi are headed to His home.

The final line of Ruth 1 says, "And they came to Bethlehem at the beginning of barley harvest" (v. 22). Barley harvest in Bethlehem represents hope and abundance for both Ruth and Naomi. Tomorrow, we'll lean in to see how.

SCRIPTURE MEMORY MOMENT

Text Hebrews 4:16 to a friend to encourage her. Share why this verse is becoming meaningful to you.

A PRAYER FOR TODAY

DEAR GOD, *thank You for the example of Ruth, who made a courageous decision to follow You. Help me to be courageous in my own life and circumstances this week. Show me places You might want to bring healing in my life. Guide my steps so I might walk toward restoration. Amen.*

DAY 4

Boaz went over and said to Ruth, "Listen, my daughter. Stay right here with us when you gather grain; don't go to any other fields. Stay right behind the young women working in my field. See which part of the field they are harvesting, and then follow them. I have warned the young men not to treat you roughly. And when you are thirsty, help yourself to the water they have drawn from the well."

Ruth fell at his feet and thanked him warmly. "What have I done to deserve such kindness?" she asked. "I am only a foreigner."

Ruth 2:8–10 NLT

Have you ever experienced a time in your life when you were an outsider and someone granted you favor or kindness? Describe what that felt like.

In Ruth 2:1, we learn some important information about a guy named Boaz. He is described as "a worthy man" (ESV) or "a man of noble character" (CSB). He is also from the same clan as Elimelech, Naomi's late husband.

After this insider detail, we return to the chronological story of Ruth and Naomi as they are first starting their new life in Bethlehem. Ruth doesn't waste any time and asks her mother-in-law's permission to go into the barley fields and glean. She hopes to find favor somewhere to help with their food shortage.

> **In day 2 of this week's lesson, we talked about God's heart for the vulnerable. Read Leviticus 19:9–10 and Deuteronomy 24:19–22. How does this instruction from God show His heart for the vulnerable?**

Gleaning was Israel's welfare system, which created an opportunity for the poor, the widow, the orphan, and the sojourner or foreigner to sustain themselves. The Mosaic gleaning law described in the verses you just read required the landowner to leave the edges of his fields unharvested. Once the harvesters were finished cutting and gathering the grain, the gleaners could gather up the remaining scraps.

Gleaning was considered a shameful way to live. It was also precarious, particularly for women, who faced danger from other hungry gleaners scrambling for the leftovers or at the hands of the hired harvesters who might take advantage of them while alone in the field.[5]

Ruth steps out in courage in an effort to provide for her mother-in-law and herself. Motivated to work and fueled by her newfound faith, Ruth arrives at a field and begins to glean. It just so happens to be Boaz's field, and it just so happens that Boaz comes from Bethlehem to visit his field on that day and sees Ruth gleaning there.

Of course, this is not actually by happenstance. This is a glorious display of God's providence, which is another major theme of the book of Ruth. The *providence of God* is defined as "the working of God's sovereignty to continually uphold, guide, and care for His creation."[6] Providence is the theological label the church has historically attached to the subject of how God governs the world. You might say it's His fingerprints on the pages of our lives.[7]

When Boaz enters his field, he greets the reapers with a hearty "The LORD be with you!" (2:4). This is a strategically placed indication that Boaz is a man of God. He immediately notices Ruth and asks his foreman about her. The foreman reveals that she is the young Moabite woman who had returned with Naomi. He also tells Boaz that Ruth has asked to glean and to gather among the sheaves after the reapers.

Don't miss this: Ruth stepped out in courage here. She proves herself a hard worker and then boldly asks if she may gather more than just the leftovers. Ruth comes from outside the Hebrew culture and presses on the measure of generosity. The foreman reports to Boaz that "she asked, 'Will you let me gather fallen grain among the bundles behind the harvesters?' She came and has been on her feet since early morning, except that she rested a little in the shelter" (Ruth 2:7 CSB). In other words, she asks to gather among the harvesters, not just at the edges of the field. Ruth is not motivated by greed but by giving.

> God has special care and provision for these four groups of people: widows, orphans, immigrants, and the poor. His heart for these vulnerable groups is threaded all throughout the Bible.

Reread Ruth 2:8–13 and continue reading verses 14–17. How does Ruth experience God's providence and abundant mercy in Boaz's field on this day?

_____

_____

_____

_____

Boaz's only obligation is to offer this foreigner the leftovers, but his kind generosity (*hesed*) shines in this moment. His immediate response is a tender word to Ruth that goes above and beyond obligation. If we do a little digging through Scripture, we discover that Boaz's mother was Rahab the prostitute, who protected Joshua's spies when they were scoping out the land in Jericho. She was a foreigner who had been invited into God's family because she trusted the God of Israel and showed kindness to His people (see Joshua 2). Boaz continues his mother's legacy of kindness.

Imagine Boaz inviting Ruth to the table for lunch that day. Ruth is coming out of poverty. She and Naomi had left Moab because they were homeless and hungry. She savors every morsel of that bread and wine vinegar he offers. The text tells us Ruth "ate until she was satisfied" (Ruth 2:14). I am sure she had grown accustomed to an empty, groaning stomach. Imagine the contrast. Boaz sends her home with a takeout box of food along with more than forty pounds of extra grain! The abundance and generosity of this meal point to several important meals in the future when God's Son, our own Redeemer, invites outsiders to His table. He was known for dining with tax collectors and women who had sordid pasts, both Jews and gentiles. He invited everyone to His table to feast on the grace served up by His Father.

Boaz also honors Ruth by inviting her to gather among the bundles of grain (Ruth 2:16–18). He offers her dignity.

How have you experienced or observed that work gives people a sense of dignity?

_____

_____

_____

_____

More than a decade ago, while I was living in the northern mountains of Haiti, I had the opportunity to help start a fair-trade jewelry business. One of the Haitian pastors and leaders of our nonprofit desired a longer-term solution for the women who often came to him begging for food and money. Many of them were widows in the church who also had children and grandchildren they were raising.

The pastor discovered a fair-trade jewelry company in Port-au-Prince that used recycled materials to craft their products. He befriended the American woman who started it, and she invited him to bring some of the women from the mountains to learn how to make jewelry. He chose a few women and sent them for training with hopes of making them leaders who would train other women in the church.

One day, as our pickup truck blazed a trail through the dust and gravel, he asked me if I would help the women start their own business. My heart leaped when I first heard his idea. I never imagined I would have the chance in Haiti to use my passion for creativity and my love for making jewelry. I grew up frequenting craft stores and creating jewelry to give as gifts to friends and family. Creativity was in my bones, and I loved the idea of sharing these skills with the women.

That summer in Haiti I gathered the first group of artisans—nine women who stepped up to learn how to roll their own beads from up-cycled cereal boxes. We formed The Haitian Bead Project. I showed them how to arrange their beads into necklaces and twist wire to make earrings. We worked together to improve the quality of our creations and to find designs that would be on trend for buyers in the United States.

By the end of the summer, we had sixty trained artisans. Teaching the women the skill of making jewelry opened up two important doors for them: the dignity of work and the power of creativity.

The dignity of work is central to our value as human beings. Work can provide a sense of purpose, honor, and hope for the future. When people develop marketable skills and find jobs, they can provide for themselves and their families. They are no longer shamed into begging and reaching for handouts.

Notice in the book of Ruth how Boaz invites Ruth to work. He is generous toward her by offering protection and opportunity, but he doesn't do all the work for her. He extends kindness and mercy, which honors her.

> **Through Ruth's trust in God and her willingness to work, she experiences God's abundance. Read Ephesians 3:20–21. How is this verse a picture of God's abundance? How does it involve you and me?**

SCRIPTURE MEMORY MOMENT

Studies show that one of the most effective ways to commit something to memory is by doing a physical activity while memorizing.[8] Work on memorizing Hebrews 4:16 while you bounce a ball, go for a walk, or dance with your kids. Say the verse out loud to help you remember it.

A PRAYER FOR TODAY

DEAR GOD, *thank You for being a God who is not far away but is intimately involved in all the details of my life. Help me see the ways You are at work on my behalf even in this present season. Show me how I can be generous and hardworking like Boaz and Ruth for the benefit of those You've placed in my family and circles. Amen.*

He said, "Who are you?" And she answered, "I am Ruth, your servant. Spread your wings over your servant, for you are a redeemer."

Ruth 3:9

Have you ever had a hard time in your life redeemed into something good? Maybe you lost a job and it was later redeemed with a better job. Or maybe you moved from a neighborhood or church and found new blessings in a new community. Share what that was like for you.

_____

_____

_____

_____

In this next scene of our story, Naomi reveals her matchmaking plans for Ruth and Boaz. Cue the soundtrack to the musical *Fiddler on the Roof.* "Matchmaker, matchmaker, make me a match . . ."

Read Ruth 3:1–13. What is Naomi's plan for redeeming Ruth's situation as a childless widow? Do you think it sounds feasible?

_____

_____

Ruth courageously steps forward once again to execute Naomi's plan. But she adds her own twist. She dresses up, heads to the dinner party at the threshing floor, and then waits until Boaz has a full, happy belly and falls asleep. Ruth uncovers his feet as Naomi instructed her and lies down.

When Boaz wakes up, he is surprised to find a woman lying there. Of course, Ruth doesn't wait quietly for his instructions like Naomi suggested. She chimes in with her own reverse marriage proposal: "I am Ruth, your servant. Spread your wings over your servant, for you are a redeemer" (Ruth 3:9). Ruth basically presents herself as eligible for marriage and uses the same metaphor Boaz had used when they first met (see 2:12) to ask him to have mercy on her. She appeals to his kindness and compassion for the vulnerable.

In his signature fashion, Boaz responds with words of blessing. He considers her proposal a "kindness" and promises to take care of everything (3:10–11). Then Boaz sends her home with six measures of barley—a detail that serves as another example of his generosity and God's abundant provision for Ruth and Naomi.

The whole story might sound like a romantic comedy, but it's actually a compelling reminder of the mercy of God, who is directing every detail. As we see Boaz step up to make the proper arrangements for

In Boaz, we get a glimpse of the ultimate Kinsman-Redeemer, Jesus Christ, who faithfully redeems every believer through His death on the cross. He paid the price for each one of us in full.

marrying Ruth, he first goes to the city gate, the place where business transactions took place in Bible times. And it just so happens that the "kinsman-redeemer" waltzes through the gate right on cue. In Hebrew culture, the kinsman-redeemer was the closest male relative who had the first option to buy Elimelech's land from Naomi. This was part of the Hebrew custom of keeping land within the tribe when a man died.

Boaz, of course, calls out to the man to come and sit down for a little chat. He also invites ten of the town's elders (aka the VIPs) to join them as witnesses.

Boaz chooses his strategy carefully. He explains the situation to the kinsman-redeemer, and at first the man expresses interest in redeeming the land. Then Boaz explains that if the guy buys the land from Naomi, he will acquire not only the land but also Ruth the Moabitess as a wife. The kinsman-redeemer will also have the responsibility to father a child with Ruth in order to continue the line of Mahlon and his father, Elimelech. After hearing this, the kinsman-redeemer quickly changes his tune and says he can't buy it after all. He knows he will ruin his own son's inheritance if he claims the right of redemption, for if Ruth were to bear a son, that child would one day inherit Elimelech's land instead of the man's son.

> Do you have a "just so happens" story? Have you ever been in just the right place at just the right time and it was obvious God orchestrated the details to get you there? Explain.

On day 1, I shared my own story about how God orchestrated every detail and Shawn answered a surprising call to marry me in a way that was similar to Boaz and Ruth's story. I'm often reminded that God was not surprised by Ericlee getting cancer. He was not surprised by his death a few months after being diagnosed. And God was working on my behalf to bring Shawn at just the right time.

Shawn gained three daughters and a wife—something he never expected or planned on. I gained a new husband and a daddy for my girls—something I never imagined could happen again. All of us together continue to live Ericlee's legacy of faith and this glory story God is writing for us. Shawn is my kinsman-redeemer, bringing surprising new value to our life and hope to our future. In the words of Naomi, we have "found rest" in this next chapter of life.

> **Reread Ruth 1:9 and 3:1 in the English Standard Version. Why do you think "rest" is a central goal for Naomi?**

At the start of the Ruth narrative, Naomi wished that Yahweh would grant "rest" to Ruth and Orpah. By that she meant that she wanted them to enjoy a life of tranquility, undisturbed by the cares, encumbrances, and troubles of widowhood.[9] Since Ruth stayed with her, Naomi sought a way to provide her with the safety and security of marriage. As a married woman, Ruth would be protected from exploitation or oppression.[10] By extension, Naomi would also be protected as her mother-in-law.

God speaks through the prophet Isaiah to challenge the people of Israel to embrace the rest He has for all of us: "For thus said the Lord GOD, the Holy One of Israel, 'In returning and rest you shall be saved; in quietness and in trust shall be your strength'" (Isa. 30:15). We can rest in God. We can trust His providence, His provision, and ultimately His mercy and grace, which are given freely. It's our choice to receive these gifts.

In her book *Sacred Rest*, Dr. Saundra Dalton-Smith explains the well-rested life this way: "It's a life lived with open hands before God, not holding on to the pain of yesterday, the blessings of today, or the promises of tomorrow, but rather trusting in God's love for you."[11]

In light of this quote, how is God calling you to rest today?

_____

_____

_____

_____

Unfortunately, we don't get all the details about Boaz and Ruth's wedding day in Ruth 4. It's basically "first comes love, then comes marriage, then comes baby in the baby carriage." But God's redemptive purposes are clearly at work for Ruth and Boaz.

Friends, let's remember that Ruth was barren for at least ten years. There was a lot of shame tied up in not being able to have children, so this is a really big deal. We see God come through as the hero of the story here, as He opens Ruth's womb and redeems her barrenness. Not only that, but Ruth and her son, Obed, are invited into the family tree of Jesus, the Messiah.

There is also redemption for Naomi in the birth of this child. We hear echoes of this in the blessing Naomi's friends from town pronounce over her in Ruth 4.

Read Ruth 4:14–15. How is Naomi's life redeemed through the marriage of Ruth and Boaz?

Back in the first chapter of the book of Ruth, Naomi returned to Bethlehem empty-handed and hungry. Now her arms and her belly are full. She has a grandson and the *hesed* of Ruth and Boaz spreading over her like wings. God has proved to be her Redeemer, covering every detail. In this, Naomi can rest.

The book of Ruth closes with a genealogy that reveals Naomi's grandson Obed was the father of Jesse, who was the father of King David himself, and from this line Jesus Christ would be born.

Ruth the Moabitess—a widowed foreigner—is grafted into God's family tree. This is a picture of ethnic reconciliation and of mercy. And God's own Son, Jesus, our ultimate Kinsman-Redeemer, is born from Ruth's branch.

In Boaz, we get a glimpse of the ultimate Kinsman-Redeemer, Jesus Christ, who faithfully redeems every believer through His death on the cross. He paid the price for each one of us in full. Like Boaz was for Ruth and Naomi, Jesus is our restorer, nourisher, and redeemer.

SCRIPTURE MEMORY MOMENT

As you are reviewing Hebrews 4:16 for this week, see if you can break up the key phrases into chunks. Practice the verse aloud with a family member or friend. See if you can say it without looking!

A PRAYER FOR TODAY

FATHER GOD, *thank You for the story of Ruth that reminds me today that You have a heart for the vulnerable and the outsider. I'm so grateful You had mercy on me and sent Your Son, Jesus, as my ultimate Kinsman-Redeemer. Help me step into the kind of soul rest that Ruth and Naomi experienced by trusting in You. Amen.*

HOW CAN WE EXTEND MERCY IN OUR EVERYDAY LIVES?

Last week we talked about the power of receiving God's mercy. We followed the story of Ruth and how God gave her the gift of mercy. In receiving His mercy, she was able to multiply it to others. This week we are going to explore how we can extend mercy to those God has placed in our everyday lives.

In today's opening story, (in)courage writer Renee Swope shares about a season when her son was embracing the ideals of atheism. This was very hard on Renee and her husband, but they chose to offer up mercy to their son instead of judgment. As you read Renee's story, think about how she accepted the opportunity to extend compassion and love to her son when he doubted, and how that made such a difference.

A Story of Mercy

In May 2013, our then fifteen-year-old son, Andrew, told us he was an atheist. The cheerful, encouraging boy we knew and loved had been fading away for months, but we couldn't get him to tell us why. Now we knew.

Although we were shocked and devastated, my husband, J.J., and I stayed calm in front of Andrew. God helped us respond in a way that Andrew would feel safe enough to be honest about his doubts and questions. We didn't want to make it about us and what we wanted. We didn't want him to feel shamed or guilted into agreeing and following God according to our terms.

Instead, we asked Andrew questions to help us understand. Later, when we were alone in our bedroom, we let all our feelings, questions, confusion, fears, and concerns come out, with God and each other.

We brainstormed together and talked about taking away YouTube, since he told us he had been watching debates between Christian and atheist scholars. J.J. wanted to convince Andrew to read books by skeptics who had become Christians. I wanted to pull him out of his current school environment and create a bubble where other teenagers couldn't influence his beliefs.

But we didn't do any of that.

We sensed God telling us not to push the Bible or our beliefs on him. Andrew had heard both his whole life. We also knew if we said too much or pushed too hard, we might push him away. And that was the last thing we wanted to do. This had to be his journey and his faith.

Andrew's journey was filled with doubts and hard questions about God, which were compounded by frustration and uncertainties about his purpose in life. It was a painful journey that broke my heart and brought me to my knees. But while I prayed for Andrew, God's grace and mercy poured over me and eventually through me to my son.

God's mercy told me not to react but to listen closely as Andrew vented—even when his words were hard to hear.

God's mercy told me to keep my mouth shut and let my actions speak louder than my emotions.

God's mercy helped me breathe deep and look for ways to affirm the unique gifts I saw in Andrew that he could no longer see in himself.

J.J. and I decided our number one priority needed to be our relationship with Andrew. We wanted home to be a safe place where he could ask hard questions. We also wanted our home to be a place where our kids felt accepted, listened to, loved, and respected as individuals.

Although we were devastated, we eventually felt deeply grateful that Andrew was still living at home when this happened. We had no idea what to say or do, but we sensed our attitude and actions were more important than our words. We prayed and sometimes begged God to intervene, having no idea how He would answer.

J.J. struggled most with feeling like a failure as a dad. I struggled most with fear. I was afraid of how far Andrew might go and how dark things might get. I had come from a family filled with alcoholism and other addictions, and I feared that without a commitment to following Jesus, he might make choices that would lead him into bondage and deep regret.

One afternoon Andrew and I were driving home from school, and I was talking to him about my concerns. I told him I wasn't going to push him toward God, but I was going to pull him away from darkness if I saw him getting too close. When I stopped talking, Andrew said, "Mom, if you believed God is as strong and powerful as you always told me He was, then you wouldn't be afraid."

He was right. My faith was being tested like never before. That afternoon when we got home, I went to my room and cried. I told Jesus I did believe, and I cried out to Him in my unbelief. I was desperate to see Him work in ways only He could. This season of parenting almost crushed me, but somehow it also strengthened me.

After a year and a half, Andrew came home from school one day and casually told me a friend had asked him if he was still an atheist. He told him, "No."

This was the first I'd heard of Andrew's heart change. I tried not to make a big deal about it and just responded with, "*Really?*"

"Yep, I told him that I got tired of living without hope! So I've given my life to Christ, and I want to give Him a chance," Andrew explained.

It came down to hope. Hope is what Andrew wanted. And hope is what he found in a personal relationship with Jesus Christ. It wasn't because we said the right things or took away all the bad things. There was so much more than we could see or do.

I believe the most important thing we did was let Andrew find his own faith and his own way to the heart of God while we focused on our relationship with our son and our relationship with Jesus. It was only through our dependence on the Father, Son, and Holy Spirit to reveal Himself to us and through us that J.J. and I were empowered to love Andrew unconditionally, pursue him relentlessly, accept him lovingly, and extend mercy and grace to him daily. God's mercy empowers us to show mercy.

—RENEE SWOPE

Have you ever struggled with doubt about your faith or walked alongside someone who was navigating doubt? Share about that experience.

Read Jude verses 20—23 below. Circle every time the word _mercy_ is used in this passage. How would you describe mercy based on these verses?

> But you, beloved, building yourselves up in your most holy faith and praying in the Holy Spirit, keep yourselves in the love of God, waiting for the mercy of our Lord Jesus Christ that leads to eternal life. And have mercy on those who doubt; save others by snatching them out of the fire; to others show mercy with fear, hating even the garment stained by the flesh.

···

···

···

···

Jude, the half brother of Jesus, is writing to fellow believers in this letter. His goal is to encourage them to contend for the faith and to multiply mercy, peace, and love (see vv. 1–2). In verses 20–23, Jude uses the
word *mercy* three times. He first talks about "waiting for the mercy of
our Lord Jesus Christ," which refers to the return or second coming of
Jesus. This mercy is something we wait for and cling to with hope.

Revelation 22:12–13 details Jesus's return: "Look, I am coming soon,
bringing my reward with me to repay all people according to their
deeds. I am the Alpha and the Omega, the First and the Last, the Beginning and the End" (NLT). Jesus was merciful toward us in dying
on the cross and will be merciful in returning one day.

Then Jude reminds his readers to "have mercy on those who doubt."
The Greek word translated as "mercy" in this verse is *eleeō*, meaning
to have pity or compassion for the miserable.[1] Jude calls us to have
compassion on those who are vacillating or going back and forth in
what they believe.

This is where Renee's son Andrew was struggling. He was listening to
debates between Christian and atheist scholars, becoming confused
about what he had grown up believing. Every Christian has doubts
about faith at one point or another. Jude reminds us in verse 22 not to
judge or be condescending toward doubters, but instead to extend compassionate mercy seasoned with love like Renee and her husband did.

Jude's final urging in this passage is to "show mercy with fear," which
may mean being cautious when engaging with those who are listening to false teachings. The doubter or one who is against God could

mislead the person attempting to help them. It's good to show active compassion toward those who doubt, but also to be cautious and exhibit a reverence and fear of God.[2]

SCRIPTURE MEMORY MOMENT

This week's memory verse is Matthew 5:7, which is part of a section of Scripture called the Beatitudes. These verses are the opening of Jesus's Sermon on the Mount, which is one of the most well-known biblical texts. Jesus used the Beatitudes to explain His personhood and His ministry, which are both characterized by humility and confidence in God. Write out Matthew 5:7 in your journal (from the CSB as printed below or from your favorite translation), and begin to meditate on these words.

Blessed are the merciful,
for they will be shown mercy.

A PRAYER FOR TODAY

DEAR LORD, *help me deepen my understanding of mercy this week. I want to be a woman who is quick to be merciful and loving to others when they are doubting and struggling. May You continue to guide me to be both humble and confident as I trust in You. Amen.*

One day an expert in religious law stood up to test Jesus by asking him this question: "Teacher, what should I do to inherit eternal life?"

Jesus replied, "What does the law of Moses say? How do you read it?"

The man answered, "'You must love the Lord your God with all your heart, all your soul, all your strength, and all your mind.' And, 'Love your neighbor as yourself.'"

"Right!" Jesus told him. "Do this and you will live!"

The man wanted to justify his actions, so he asked Jesus, "And who is my neighbor?"

Luke 10:25–29 NLT

Who do you consider as your neighbor? (Hint: It doesn't have to be someone who lives next door.)

What was the motive of the religious leader who stood up to question Jesus in Luke 10:25–29? How do you think this influenced his questions?

> God's mercy empowers us to show mercy.
>
> —RENEE SWOPE

This religious leader who questioned Jesus was probably a Pharisee who wanted to challenge Jesus and justify his own good deeds. Jesus knows He is talking to an expert in the law (Torah), so He asks the man to identify what the law says about eternal life. The man responds by quoting two Old Testament commandments from Deuteronomy 6:5 and Leviticus 19:18. Let's consider these commandments in their original context.

Deuteronomy 6:5 is part of what is known as the Shema (from the Hebrew word for "hear" in Deut. 6:4), and it comes after Moses has repeated the Ten Commandments to the people. Deuteronomy 6:5–6 says, "Love the LORD your God with all your heart, with all your soul, and with all your strength. These words that I am giving you today are to be in your heart" (CSB). The implication here is that God's commandments are not just a checklist of dos and don'ts, but rather guidelines to train our hearts and then inform our actions.

The expert in the law then quotes a snippet of Leviticus 19:18 as the second idea that leads to eternal life: "You shall not take vengeance or bear a grudge against the sons of your own people, but you shall *love your neighbor as yourself*: I am the LORD" (emphasis added). This commandment is important to us today because it helps summarize how we are to live and engage with others. Our attitudes and actions should be motivated by love and compassion. We naturally care for ourselves and our own well-being. We need to have this same kind of care and regard for our neighbors.

Then the man asks Jesus this poignant question: "And who is my neighbor?" (Luke 10:29).

Jesus answers him with a parable (or story) to illustrate.

> **Read Luke 10:30—37. Name the three people who saw the man who'd been attacked on the road. How would you characterize these people or who might they represent in society?**

Jesus throws a twist into the story when He says the Samaritan was the one who stopped to help the man who had been attacked. Jesus knows the history between Jews and Samaritans, who held a mutual disdain for each other. Jews considered themselves pure descendants of Abraham and did not accept the Samaritans as part of their community because the Samaritans were a mixed race. After the northern kingdom of Israel was destroyed and its people carried off by the Assyrians in 722 BC, those Israelites who were left behind intermarried with non-Jewish people from the surrounding nations, and the Samaritans were their descendants. The Samaritans worshiped Yahweh and used the Pentateuch (the first five books of the Bible) as their Scriptures, but they worshiped on Mount Gerizim instead of at the temple in Jerusalem. The Jews discriminated against them for where they worshiped and because of their ethnically mixed background.

Does that sound like something that creeps up between different religious groups—or worse, among Christian denominations—in our modern times? We so often get caught up in where, how, and when people worship. We are quick to judge a music style or choice of dress and justify not helping or partnering with someone because of it.

Maybe Jesus is challenging us to think about our neighbor as more than just the people who live near us, who we schedule playdates with for our kids, or who we sit next to at church. Our neighbor could be the person who voted for that other political candidate, someone with a different skin tone or cultural heritage, or someone from a different income bracket.

How does the parable of the good Samaritan expand your understanding of "neighbor"? Brainstorm more specific examples that might be outside your comfort zone of people you might consider as your neighbor. What people in your city, workplace, or sphere of influence might be your neighbors?

_____

_____

_____

_____

Have you ever held back from helping someone because you were on your way to something else important? Or have you ever turned away from helping someone in need because you were fearful about the situation? I am sad to admit I have.

In his "I Have Been to the Mountaintop" speech, delivered in Memphis, Tennessee, just before he was assassinated in 1968, Dr. Martin Luther King Jr. referenced the parable of the good Samaritan. Dr. King speculated that maybe the priest and the Levite were too busy or fearful, and that's why they didn't immediately stop to help the man:

> And you know, it's possible that the priest and the Levite looked over that man on the ground and wondered if the robbers were still around. Or it's possible that they felt that the man on the ground was

merely faking. And he was acting like he had been robbed and hurt, in order to seize them over there, lure them there for quick and easy seizure. And so, the first question that the priest asked—the first question that the Levite asked was, "If I stop to help this man, what will happen to me?" But then the Good Samaritan came by. And he reversed the question: "If I do not stop to help this man, what will happen to him?"[3]

What a selfless and merciful way to reframe the question! The parable of the good Samaritan challenged the religious leaders and all those who heard Jesus's teaching to consider the man in need rather than themselves. What a good challenge for us today as we are asking God to create a heart of mercy in us!

Read 1 John 3:16—18. How does Christ's sacrifice serve as an example of the way we should show love and mercy to others?

_____

_____

_____

_____

SCRIPTURE MEMORY MOMENT

Write Matthew 5:7 on an index card or sticky note. Tape it in a place you will see it often, such as your car dashboard, the window above your kitchen sink, or your bathroom mirror. Be sure to read it throughout the week.

A PRAYER FOR TODAY

DEAR JESUS, *I am challenged today to consider who my neighbor is. Please use this week to deepen my understanding of this question, and open my heart if I need to expand my definition of neighbor. Show me how to love You and love my neighbor with a greater measure of mercy and grace. Amen.*

All this is from God, who through Christ reconciled us to himself and gave us the ministry of reconciliation; that is, in Christ God was reconciling the world to himself, not counting their trespasses against them, and entrusting to us the message of reconciliation. Therefore, we are ambassadors for Christ, God making his appeal through us. We implore you on behalf of Christ, be reconciled to God.

2 Corinthians 5:18–20

Describe a time when you experienced reconciliation or witnessed two people reconciling.

_____

_____

_____

_____

Reconciliation means settling a disagreement or reuniting with someone we have been alienated from. Reconciliation requires that both parties accept the terms of the settlement. Sometimes we have to make amends or compensate a person for any loss, damage, or injury they have experienced. Reconciliation can happen between sisters, friends, neighbors, coworkers, and others. Forgiveness can lead to this kind of restored fellowship.

The concept of reconciliation is central to the gospel. Sin separated us from God. Then God did what we could not do: He credited or transferred our sins to His sinless Son as a mediator so that we could be reconciled or reunited with Him. It's like God issued a peace treaty to us that was signed in the blood of His Son who died in our place. God made this sacrifice out of His great mercy for us. We are called to be generous with mercy as He's been generous with us.

> **Read 2 Corinthians 5:18–20. How would you describe the ministry of reconciliation based on these verses?**

These verses remind us that mercy and grace are gifts from God. As those who have received God's mercy and grace, we are called to be arrows pointing others back to God. Paul reminds us in 1 Timothy 2:4 that God desires for all people to hear and understand the gospel so they have the opportunity to believe it and receive eternal life.

Once we have been adopted into God's family as believers, He can use us as ambassadors to others, representatives of His truth. When we choose to reconcile or be unified with others who are different from us, our unity can be our testimony.

> **Are there people in your life with whom you need to make amends or pursue reconciliation? How can you show them mercy and reach out to them today?**

Our neighbor could be the person who voted for that other political candidate, someone with a different skin tone or cultural heritage, or someone from a different income bracket.

Now let's return to the parable of the good Samaritan. Reread Luke 10:30–37, keeping in mind what we have learned about God's mercy and grace toward us.

What specific things does the Samaritan do for the wounded man? Why are these significant?

In the parable, Jesus emphasizes the Samaritan's generosity. The Samaritan doesn't owe the wounded man anything, but he is moved by compassion and extends generous mercy across cultural lines when he sees a person in need.

In her book *Open Hands, Willing Heart*, Vivian Mabuni points out that Jesus made the hated Samaritan the hero of the story. This would have been jarring for the Jewish listeners. The culturally hated man acted with generosity and love. As verse 37 emphasizes, the Samaritan was "the one who showed him mercy." Mabuni writes, "Part of having a heart willing to bend to God's will is stepping up to address differences and injustices, understanding that we are responding to God's image bearers. This isn't a political issue; it's a *gospel* issue Jesus taught about regularly. As Christians we are called to the ministry of reconciliation."[4]

Yesterday we considered the question "Who is my neighbor?" Mabuni challenges us to think about our neighbor who may be from a different cultural or racial background or who is enduring some kind of injustice. We are called not only to love that person but also to stand up for, defend, and care for her.

> Is there someone in your everyday life who is from a different cultural or racial heritage who might need your care today? Describe them below. Spend some time in prayer and ask God to show you what caring for them and offering mercy might look like.

SCRIPTURE MEMORY MOMENT

Test yourself on Matthew 5:7. Try to say it out loud and write it from memory. Set it to a little tune you can sing in the car or while you're doing dishes. Hide these words in your heart as you continue to reflect on them.

A PRAYER FOR TODAY

DEAR GOD, *I'm deeply grateful for Your generosity toward me. Thank You for the times You have welcomed me back into Your arms even when I have been unfaithful or distracted. Show me ways I can extend mercy instead of judgment toward others in my family and circles of influence this week. Amen.*

And if you do good to those who do good to you, what benefit is that to you? For even sinners do the same. And if you lend to those from whom you expect to receive, what credit is that to you? Even sinners lend to sinners, to get back the same amount. But love your enemies, and do good, and lend, expecting nothing in return, and your reward will be great, and you will be sons of the Most High, for he is kind to the ungrateful and the evil. Be merciful, even as your Father is merciful.

Luke 6:33–36

Is it challenging for you to give without expecting something in return? Why or why not?

In Luke 6, Jesus gives honor to the poor, the hungry, the grieving, and the hated. He reminds them that their reward in heaven will be great. Then He goes on to share about how the roles of the rich and poor will be reversed in God's future kingdom.

Jesus urges His listeners, "Love your enemies, do what is good to those who hate you, bless those who curse you, pray for those who mistreat you" (Luke 6:27–28 CSB). He emphasizes love, charity, and goodness as traits that should characterize the people of God. Jesus sets God's character as the ethical standard for all people.

> **Look up the following verses and write down what you learn about God's character from them:**
>
> Leviticus 19:2
> Deuteronomy 10:17–18
> Psalm 25:8–10
> Matthew 5:48

In many ways, it's counterintuitive for us to love our neighbors, especially if they are hard to be around. As humans, we want to protect ourselves. We don't want to do good for people who insult us or pray for those who mistreat us. We would much rather hang out with people who smell good, who receive us well, and who praise us. It might be hard for us to love the neighbor who hosts loud parties that keep our children awake late at night, or to cover a shift for a coworker we heard gossiping about us, or to embrace the person who doesn't look or act like us at church.

And yet, Jesus came for the sick, not for the well (see Matt. 9:12–13). He came for those in need. He came for the outcasts of society and the sinners, not for those who were bent on justifying themselves. He came for the people who were challenging to be around, not the ones who were winning the popularity or beauty contests.

I remember several summers ago I flew to Chicago and rode the train to the neighborhood on the south side where I grew up. I decided to grab lunch at a little Italian place where I once worked as a waitress. More than eighteen years had passed since I had laid eyes on those tables with checkered tablecloths, and I was feeling nostalgic as I sat there waiting for my Italian beef sandwich.

I noticed a woman wander in. She had ashy skin and wore slouchy, threadbare clothes. She started asking the waitress for the lasagna she had supposedly ordered a few days earlier but never picked up. The waitress kept telling her she needed to see a receipt. The woman clearly didn't have a receipt.

I knew in my heart this was my opportunity. The woman and I locked eyes. She came over and asked if she could use my phone to call her aunt for a ride. I was about to hand over my phone but then thought twice and asked if I could make the call for her. She told me her name was Mary and gave me her aunt's number. When the woman picked up and I explained that Mary was with me, she said she was at work and Mary needed to wait until she was done if she needed a ride. She whispered that Mary had some mental health challenges.

I hung up and relayed most of that information to Mary. Just then the waitress delivered my food. I saw Mary's eyes hover over the bag and the giant lemonade in my hand. I headed for the door, and she followed me. Just outside the door, I turned to her and asked her if she'd like to share my lunch. Her eyes lit up and she nodded.

As I dug in the bag for my sandwich, the waitress and manager came out. They told me I didn't need to give Mary food and apologized for the inconvenience. I froze, unsure of what to do next. "We'll make her something," the waitress assured me. I searched her eyes to see if she was sincere.

Somewhere between that phone call and the door, Mary had crossed the threshold of my heart. I knew she was mine to care for that day. I pulled out my wallet and handed the waitress a twenty-dollar bill. "Get her what she wants for lunch, please," I said.

The server thanked me. The manager stood watching, incredulous. Somewhat embarrassed by the attention, I turned to leave. Then Mary called after me in her husky voice, "Can I give you a hug?"

I paused. I ran back to her and hugged her neck tightly. "God bless you," she whispered.

Have you ever been in a situation where you were compelled to love someone even if it felt awkward or uncomfortable? What did you do?

Read 1 John 4:19. What should compel us to love others? Does this perspective help you to love the people in your life who feel unlovable?

Here's the deal: I pulled a twenty-dollar bill out of my wallet. I spend at least ten times that each month eating out with my family, so the financial sacrifice was minimal. But in that moment the Holy Spirit was at work fine-tuning my perspective.

The first shift for me was in remembering that it's not my place to judge how someone uses the gift I give. So often I find myself in a quandary over whether to give someone money that I end up doing nothing at all. I get stuck wondering about whether they will use that money to buy drugs or alcohol. My mind winds through a labyrinth, wondering if by giving them money I'm somehow perpetuating their addictions or problems. The reality is that this could happen, but I'm learning it's not my job to predict if someone will be responsible or not. I am not to judge. Discernment is good but should never be an excuse for complacency.

Instead, I can dig deeper and see if the person in my path has a more specific need beyond money. Of course, that requires going a step further and taking time to ask what they need. I may discover they really need a meal, a warm blanket, or a pair of shoes. Sometimes engaging with a person may even require me to learn more about policy issues and how I can be an advocate for affordable housing or job training.

Rather than a pat-myself-on-the-back moment, this was a stoop-lower opportunity. I became acutely aware that feeding Mary, offering her dignity through a smile or hug, was not about charity or me changing the world as much as it was about obedience to the gospel.

Read Matthew 25:35–40. Write out a prayer to God in light of what you have read and learned about mercy today.

SCRIPTURE MEMORY MOMENT

Don't underestimate the power of movement while memorizing. Go for a short walk in your neighborhood or even around your office while reciting Matthew 5:7. Say the words out loud or to a certain cadence if that helps you.

A PRAYER FOR TODAY

DEAR JESUS, *thank You for Your patience with me this week. I ask that You continue to mold and move my heart toward Your will—even if it feels uncomfortable. Help me reframe my perspective in areas where I might be selfish or afraid so I can act on the promptings You give. Create in me a heart of mercy. Amen.*

DAY 5

Those who consider themselves religious and yet do not keep a tight rein on their tongues deceive themselves, and their religion is worthless. Religion that God our Father accepts as pure and faultless is this: to look after orphans and widows in their distress and to keep oneself from being polluted by the world.

James 1:26–27 NIV

What images come to mind when you think about those who are helpless in your community and around the world?

_____

_____

_____

_____

Read James 1:26–27. What do you think the word _religious_ means in these verses?

_____

_____

_____

_____

James, a half brother of Jesus, is writing to Jewish believers about how Christians are to live out their faith. He wants his audience to be "doers of the word and not hearers only" (James 1:22 CSB).

James redefines what it means to be religious by explaining some of the ways we should practice our faith and show our devotion to Christ. Let's remember that James himself was once a skeptic, but through a personal encounter with the risen Jesus, he became a believer and eventually a leader in the early church. In his letter, he gives us a practical, how-to resource on Christian living.

Read James 1:27 in a few different translations in your Bible app or at BibleStudyTools.com. What do you discover? Does the wording from any of these versions help you better understand the spirit of this verse?

What two practices of "pure and faultless religion" does James describe? Why do you think James specifically names orphans and widows in this verse?

James mentions two classes of people in his culture who had the fewest rights, the least hope, and the greatest vulnerability. These were not the only vulnerable people in that culture; rather, they represent all people who need help and compassion.

One summer when my family was living in Haiti, I found my four-year-old outside our back door with a box of Band-Aids. She was surrounded by a group of kids from the orphanage. Every one of them was sporting a Dora the Explorer Band-Aid and a huge grin.

"What are you doing, love?" I asked nonchalantly.

"I'm putting Band-Aids on all their boo-boos," she responded with great purpose.

For a split second, I thought about getting upset with her for using the entire box of Band-Aids her grandma had given her. We probably wouldn't be able to get more for several weeks. But when I looked into those kids' eyes and saw their pure delight as each one admired their Dora Band-Aid, I couldn't be mad.

My daughter had offered those kids a great gift. She saw each one of them as important, as human, as friends worthy of her special Dora Band-Aids. She was on a mission to bind up their wounds. Truth be told, maybe only one of those kids was actually bleeding or had a wound that required a Band-Aid. Yet my girl's generosity and compassion challenged me in a profound way. She was growing a heart of mercy, and it compelled her to serve her friends.

Mercy is a practice, a discipline of extending kindness we receive from God to those around us. It's a practice of seeing people through God's eyes of compassion and being moved to action.

Mercy is a practice of seeing people through God's eyes of compassion and being moved to action.

In big and small ways, we are invited into the practice of mercy every day. One day it might be offering a Band-Aid to a friend with a skinned knee. The next day it might be giving a neighbor a ride to the doctor or watching a single mom's kids so she can attend a meeting. Maybe it's resisting the urge to retaliate when someone criticizes us or to make an unsavory comment when someone cuts us off in traffic. Or maybe it's donating to a relief fund following a tragedy or signing up to sponsor a child through a nonprofit organization that will provide them with food and education.

Renee and her husband showed mercy toward their son in this week's opening story. The Good Samaritan showed mercy toward the man who lay dying on the road. And Jesus showed mercy toward each one of us by offering us forgiveness on the cross rather than judgment.

> Read 1 Thessalonians 5:14–18. Paul encourages his brothers and sisters in the faith at Thessalonica and guides them to live like Christ in a culture that is opposed to Christian ideas. According to this passage, what is the will of God? How does this inspire you to show mercy in new ways?

SCRIPTURE MEMORY MOMENT

Today is the last day for working on Matthew 5:7. Practice the verse aloud with a family member or friend. See if you can say it without looking!

A PRAYER FOR TODAY

DEAR JESUS, *thank You for the invitation to partner with You to offer mercy to those in need. Open my eyes to the needs of orphans, widows, and others who need help in my community. Help me seek out opportunities to serve others as an offering of thanksgiving for the mercy You've shown me. Amen.*

HOW DO MERCY AND JUSTICE COEXIST?

Friends, thank you for sticking with me on this journey toward cultivating a heart of mercy. So far we have explored what mercy is, why we need mercy, how we receive mercy, and how to extend mercy to others in our everyday lives. This week we will look at the intersection of mercy and justice. Let's ponder this question together: How can God be both just and merciful at the same time?

In today's opening story, (in)courage writer Michelle Ami Reyes shares about a situation her church in Austin, Texas, faced when a member of the community needed both help and mercy. As you read Michelle's story, resist the urge to judge the person she describes. Instead, take note of how the church responded and the effect that had on the man and his family.

A Story of Mercy

"I need your help. My brother is in trouble."

These were the first words out of a dear sister's mouth when she came over one afternoon. From the way her hands shook and her eyes stayed fixed on the ground, I knew it was no easy thing for her to come to me for help. Where we live in East Austin, folks don't air their family's dirty laundry—it's considered a betrayal of family trust. If this woman had decided to ask for help, she was truly desperate.

As I listened to my friend's story, I realized the situation was complicated. Isn't it always? Her brother was on the run. He had done something wrong, driven to desperation by poverty, joblessness, even the threat of homelessness. He was a vulnerable man—a poor, ethnic minority in the inner city who had endured much injustice himself and was now doing whatever he thought he could to care for his family. He was in need of compassion and help, but the wrongs he committed needed to be addressed too.

I quickly found myself praying as I listened to my friend. I needed God's wisdom. I couldn't just come down with a heavy hand of judgment. It's hard to know how to love and care for people when the situation isn't clear-cut. Humans are complicated, and caring for one another is equally complicated. Thankfully, we have a God who balances mercy and justice and who knows exactly how to care for us even in our greatest messes.

I think about the great troublemakers in the Bible. Folks like Jacob, who stole his brother's birthright and lied to his father. Or Tamar, who tricked her father-in-law into having a child with her so that she wouldn't become marginalized in her society. Human error and God's providence go hand in hand in these stories. There are so many circumstances that drive people to desperate measures. They lie, cheat, and steal to survive. Such has always been the plight of the least of these. Yet God in His mercy does not smite us. In fact, both Jacob and Tamar are in the lineage of Jesus, and Tamar is praised for her righteousness.

Sounds upside down, doesn't it? But that's how our just and merciful God chooses to work. He sees the hurting, the vulnerable, the marginalized and creates good from their mess. That's true for all of us. If we follow God, He deals with our sin while also generously inviting us back into life with Him.

In the same way that we have been shown mercy, God asks us to extend mercy to others. I'm not talking about overlooking serious criminal offenses. When there are issues of violence and abuse, the authorities should be contacted. The mercy I'm talking about is in line with Matthew 5:7, where Jesus says, "Blessed are the merciful for they shall receive mercy." To be merciful means we intentionally choose to not be harsh or derogatory in our response to others. It means that we show compassion and empathy. Even if a wrong must be addressed, we do so while treating the other person as one created in the image of God, deserving of dignity and worth. The more we understand our own mess and the wrongs we've committed, the more we can be gracious toward the messes of others.

Mercy doesn't negate justice. However, mercy compels us to pursue restorative justice over punitive justice. In other words, we are called to care for the whole person—their heart and well-being. Especially when it comes to the hurting and the marginalized in our communities, the ultimate goal must be restoration: spiritual restoration between that person and God, relational restoration between that person and their family or community, and communal restoration between that person and society. That, too, is justice.

After my friend shared her burden with me, my husband and I eventually got in touch with her brother. As we began to get to know him better, we also talked with him about the consequences of his actions and what was required to restore the safety and stability of his family. We didn't shame him. We didn't insult him or pour on guilt. He knew what he had done was wrong.

Instead, our posture was to show this young man that we cared for him, we cared about his life, we were for him, and God loved him. In some ways that was challenging, but we made it clear from the beginning that we wanted to know his story. We wanted to know what he had been through and what pushed him to the point of doing something so desperate. More than that, mercy meant responding to his story with the words, "We hear you and we acknowledge the pain of what you've been through."

If we are following the model of Christ, mercy and justice require one final step. When we recognize a person's brokenness, mercy and justice compel us to give that person another chance, because no one is beyond redemption. I love the way Matt Mikalatos explains love and mercy in his book *Journey to Love*: "To love someone fully requires not only that we know and love what is broken and worst about them, but that we love them despite those things."[1]

True love, true mercy is seeing the whole person, knowing their wrongs, and choosing not to keep any record of those wrongs (1 Cor. 13:5). That kind of mercy runs counter to our natural instincts!

There's no magic formula for how we should respond to every perceived offense. Each person and situation is different and will require a nuanced response. I do know that whatever the issue, we can approach it with a posture of justice balanced with mercy. We can challenge ourselves to not discuss justice in some theoretical form but rather to know real people and real stories and to extend biblical compassion and love for our fellow image bearers. Most importantly, we must ask, *What does restoration look like?*

May our witness as followers of Jesus run countercultural to the ways of this world, and may people see God's mercy and justice through our compassion and care for broken, hurting individuals and communities.

—MICHELLE AMI REYES

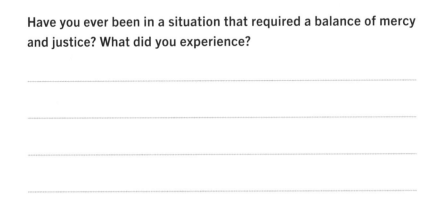

Have you ever been in a situation that required a balance of mercy and justice? What did you experience?

We concluded last week by looking at a passage from James 1 about showing mercy, especially to the vulnerable people in our communities such as widows and orphans. In chapter 2, James warns against the sin of favoritism and points his audience to the law of love. He asks this poignant question: "My dear brothers and sisters, how can you claim to have faith in our glorious Lord Jesus Christ if you favor some people over others?" (James 2:1 NLT).

Then James goes on to challenge his audience to think about the ways they favor the rich over the poor. The rich are often given the seat of honor or excused from sin, while the poor are often accused, overlooked, or put in a proverbial corner.

James follows up with two more questions: "Listen to me, dear brothers and sisters. Hasn't God chosen the poor in this world to be rich in faith? Aren't they the ones who will inherit the Kingdom he promised to those who love him?" (James 2:5 NLT). As theologian Tony Evans explains, "James's main point here is that if you practice discrimination against those made in the image of God, you're guilty of sin no matter how many rules you follow."[2]

> **Read James 2:12–13 in the ESV. What do you think the phrase "mercy triumphs over judgment" means in this context?**

It's tempting to put ourselves in the judgment seat, but we are to leave judgment to God because each person will stand before Him one day. We are asked to offer up mercy and compassion toward those in need, pointing them always toward redemption and restoration through faith in Jesus Christ.

As you think about the call to "love your neighbor as yourself," how could loving others with mercy be freeing for us?

_____

_____

_____

_____

SCRIPTURE MEMORY MOMENT

In your journal, write out Isaiah 30:18 (as printed below from the English Standard Version or from your favorite translation). Commit these words to memory this week as you think about how mercy and justice complement each other.

> *Therefore the LORD waits to be gracious to you,*
> *and therefore he exalts himself to show mercy*
> *to you.*
> *For the LORD is a God of justice;*
> *blessed are all those who wait for him.*

A PRAYER FOR TODAY

DEAR LORD, *thank You for Your forgiveness and love, which cover over all of our sins. Help me refrain from judging others and instead listen for ways You are guiding me to show them mercy. Jesus, thank You for not shaming me when I fall short. Help me to offer the same grace to others. Amen.*

Is not this the kind of fasting I have chosen:
to loose the chains of injustice
    and untie the cords of the yoke,
to set the oppressed free
    and break every yoke?
Is it not to share your food with the hungry
    and to provide the poor wanderer with shelter—
when you see the naked, to clothe them,
    and not to turn away from your own flesh and blood?
Then your light will break forth like the dawn,
    and your healing will quickly appear;
then your righteousness will go before you,
    and the glory of the Lord will be your rear guard.

Isaiah 58:6–8 NIV

**What images or practices do you think of when you hear the word
fasting?**

The initial audience for the book of Isaiah was the nation of Judah living in Jerusalem before the Babylonian conquest and exile. In Isaiah 58, the prophet describes the people's hypocrisy in their approach to fasting and calls them to repentance. Fasting was typically connected with abstaining from food and drink for a set amount of time with the purpose of increasing one's hunger for God and sharpening focus on Him.

Isaiah calls out the people because they were fasting only for selfish reasons and to show they had checked religious boxes. He then illustrates the kind of fasting God is interested in.

> **Read Isaiah 58:6–10. What examples of fasting does God prefer based on these verses? Why do you think these were important to God?**

For people accustomed to placing value only on those with power and affluence, Isaiah's words certainly would have been unexpected! Through this prophecy, God makes it clear that He will not be manipulated into showing favor or grace toward people. He is most concerned with the motivation of our hearts. These verses display God's heart for justice for the poor and oppressed. As Michelle highlighted in her story yesterday, our witness as believers in Christ should run countercultural to the ways of this world. We are invited to follow Jesus's example and extend compassion and care for broken, hurting communities.

Isaiah uses poetic language about light breaking through the darkness to show the healing and blessing that come through practicing true self-denial, extending mercy, and helping those in need. These images are repeated throughout the whole chapter and provide inspiration for all of us to step into biblical justice, which involves defending the rights and tending to the needs of the poor and oppressed. God's character is rooted in justice. This is evident throughout the Old and New Testaments.

In his book *Pursuing Justice*, Ken Wytsma writes, "If we ignore justice, like ignoring love or truth, we create a caricature rather than the divine character we meet in Scripture and in our lives. Justice is a hallmark of God, a distinctive and pure feature of His character that defines Him and His will for the world."[3]

> **Read the following verses and summarize what they show you about God's heart for justice.**
>
> Psalm 11:7
> Proverbs 14:21
> Proverbs 31:8–9
> Isaiah 5:16
> Amos 5:22–24

These verses give us a window into how justice is important to God. Let's drill down a little further into what justice means and how it's related to mercy. When people think of the word *justice* in the context of our judicial system, they may be thinking about punitive

> When we recognize a person's brokenness, mercy and justice compel us to give that person another chance, because no one is beyond redemption.
>
> —MICHELLE AMI REYES

justice, which focuses more on punishment to deter crime. A court of law determines what is true and fair and the necessary punishment for breaking the law.

Biblical justice has a broader meaning that involves special concern for the vulnerable. It is restorative in that it seeks to restore a person's understanding that they are an image bearer of God.

Genesis 1:27 says that each one of us is created in God's image. This does not mean we are gods but that we were created by God to be like Him and reflect His glory to the world. In his book *Generous Justice*, Timothy Keller writes, "The sacredness of God has in some ways been imparted to humanity, so that every human life is sacred and every human being has dignity."[4] Every human being has value and should be treated as valuable.

Now let's look at a New Testament passage that echoes what we read in Isaiah 58. In Matthew 23, Jesus shares a message about practicing what we preach. He tells the crowds to follow the commands of the scribes and Pharisees but not to follow their actions.[5] He then proclaims seven "woes" or warnings specifically for the religious leaders. One of these is particularly relevant to our conversation about justice and mercy today: "Woe to you, scribes and Pharisees, hypocrites! For you tithe mint and dill and cumin, and have neglected the weightier matters of the law: justice and mercy and faithfulness. These you ought to have done, without neglecting the others" (Matt. 23:23).

This is strong language, but Jesus is driving home the point that His Father cares deeply about justice, mercy, and faithfulness. These are not minor to God. He's tired of the leaders boasting about how they tithe on everything (even their herbs!) and making a public show out of fasting while oppressing the vulnerable in private. In Mark 12:40, for example, Jesus talks about how the religious leaders were praying lengthy, showy prayers in public but behind the scenes were taking advantage of widows' houses and land. In Matthew 21:12–13, Jesus enters the temple and overturns the tables of the money changers and those who were selling pigeons because He knew they were taking advantage of the poor. They were gouging them with low exchanges for foreign currency and high prices for animals used for sacrifices.

Read through Matthew 23:23–25. How are the scribes and Pharisees described in this passage? How do their attitudes contradict the posture described in Isaiah 58:6–8?

Friends, the reality is that mercy is messy. Michelle and her husband grappled with how to approach the situation with her friend whose brother was in trouble. They were led to show compassion for her brother by listening to his story and treating him as a fellow human being. This was part of the process of extending mercy and justice to him.

Have you ever had the chance to extend mercy by listening to someone's story? Think about someone who might have a difficult story—someone who might be navigating poverty or disease, someone who is a refugee or undocumented immigrant. Maybe it's someone who has endured an extreme trial. Did listening to their story change your heart in any way?

_____

_____

_____

_____

In Mark 5, Jesus is on His way to heal the sick daughter of a ruler of the synagogue. Along His route, He is interrupted by a woman who has suffered from bleeding for twelve years. She had spent her life savings on treatments and doctors. Many people had taken advantage of her. She reaches out to touch Jesus's garment, believing in faith that simply touching Him will bring healing. Jesus turns to heal her publicly and then invites her to share her story with those listening.

> But the woman, knowing what had happened to her, came in fear and trembling and fell down before him and told him the whole truth. And he said to her, "Daughter, your faith has made you well; go in peace, and be healed of your disease." (vv. 33–34)

Jesus is on His way to heal someone else, but He allows for this interruption and offers this woman respect and healing. He extends mercy and justice by seeing her in her distress and vulnerability, healing her from the bleeding, and inviting her to share her whole story. His compassion shows His mercy, while His willingness to stand up for her and listen to her displays His heart for justice.

SCRIPTURE MEMORY MOMENT

Write out Isaiah 30:18 on an index card or a sticky note. Read it at least three times. Place that card in a place where you can see it throughout the week.

A PRAYER FOR TODAY

DEAR JESUS, *I want to cultivate a heart like Yours that is characterized by justice and mercy. Help me take time to listen well to the stories of people around me. Show me ways I can offer dignity and help to fellow image bearers in need. Amen.*

DAY 3

One of the criminals hanging alongside cursed him: "Some Messiah you are! Save yourself! Save us!"

But the other one made him shut up: "Have you no fear of God? You're getting the same as him. We deserve this, but not him—he did nothing to deserve this."

Then he said, "Jesus, remember me when you enter your kingdom."

He said, "Don't worry, I will. Today you will join me in paradise."

Luke 23:39–43 MSG

Can you imagine being one of those criminals hanging on the cross next to Jesus? What feelings or emotions come to mind?

_____

_____

_____

_____

Read Luke 23:39–43. Why do you believe Jesus told the second criminal, "Today you will join me in paradise"? Why would he get to see Jesus in paradise?

_____

_____

_____

_____

_____

This scene from Luke 23 takes place right before the climax of Jesus's crucifixion. Of the four Gospel writers, only Luke records this moment with Jesus on the cross talking to the criminals being crucified beside Him.

Imagine this scene: Jesus has been betrayed by one of the men in His inner circle—one of His twelve disciples. Then He is arrested and taken to trial, where He is sentenced to death for claiming to be the Son of God. The Roman governor tries to convince the Jewish leaders and people that Jesus is innocent, but they deny him and form a mob. In an attempt to appease the growing mob, the governor has Jesus stripped, mocked, and severely beaten. But the mob is not satisfied and instead calls for His crucifixion.

Death by crucifixion was a sentence reserved for traitors and criminals. The Romans would use bare tree trunks on the side of the highways and purposely crucify people on the main roads going into the city to warn visitors not to defy Rome.[6] The soldiers stripped Jesus and put a scarlet robe on Him—not to honor Him but to mock Him. They twisted together a crown made of sharp thorns and pressed it onto His head. They spit on Him, flogged Him, and then forced Him to climb up a hill. He was so weak He couldn't even carry His own cross. When they got to the place called The Skull, they nailed Him to the cross, which the soldiers had forced a bystander to carry.

These are the details that lead up to the scene in Luke 23:39–43. Can you imagine the emotional, physical, and mental anguish Jesus endured? Betrayal, beatings, mocking. And yet there's this surprising moment of truth when the two criminals hanging on either side of Him talk to Jesus. They reach two different conclusions about who He is.

> **Biblical justice is restorative in that it seeks to restore a person's understanding that they are an image bearer of God.**

The first criminal joins the crowd and mocks Jesus, saying, "Are you not the Christ? Save yourself and us!"

> **Read Luke 23:40–41. How does the second criminal defend Jesus and recognize who He truly is in these verses?**

In Luke 23:43, Jesus is anticipating going to heaven and seeing the criminal redeemed. The criminal didn't expect to be released from his earthly punishment. He recognized that he deserved death for the crimes he had committed in his life. He needed to make amends on earth for what he did wrong (as we discussed in week 4, day 3). Jesus offered him mercy and forgiveness because he believed. Jesus basically says, "I'll see you there!" What an incredible gift for that man to receive the promise of heaven right before his death!

The repentant criminal recognized and believed two things: Jesus was innocent, and Jesus is the King headed to His heavenly kingdom. His declaration to Jesus made all the difference. This provides hope for all of us.

> **Read Romans 3:23–24 and 2 Corinthians 5:21. How do these New Testament verses further reinforce Jesus Christ's role for you?**

Although all of us have sinned and fall short of the glory of God, the death we deserved for our sins was transferred to God's beloved Son. We are spared from the punishment we deserve (Rom. 5:6–11).

An understanding of Jesus Christ as the one who stepped up to be a substitute for us is critical to our faith. In the Old Testament, animals were offered as a sacrifice to obtain forgiveness of sins. Yet these sacrifices could never fully atone for sin. Jesus Christ secured complete and permanent forgiveness for our sins by dying on the cross and rising from the dead. The fancy seminary term for that is *substitutionary atonement*. In Jesus, both justice and mercy were brought together when He paid the price for our sins.

The Old Testament prophet Isaiah gives us a detailed description of Jesus as the "suffering servant." Isaiah 53 was written hundreds of years before the birth of Christ but gives specific details about His crucifixion and death. Jesus's sacrifice for us was redemptive.

Read Isaiah 53:5–6. In light of what you have learned today, write out a prayer thanking God for sacrificing His Son and embodying justice and mercy for you and me.

SCRIPTURE MEMORY MOMENT

Text Isaiah 30:18 to a friend. Try to type it out from memory first and then double-check it in your Bible. Add a word of encouragement for your friend or share what you are learning.

A PRAYER FOR TODAY

DEAR JESUS, *I am humbled by the sacrifice You made for me on the cross. Thank You for volunteering as a substitute and suffering for all of us. Like the repentant criminal, I ask for Your forgiveness. I am anticipating seeing You in heaven one day. Show me how I can point others to Your saving grace. Amen.*

He has shown you, O mortal, what is good.
    And what does the LORD require of you?
To act justly and to love mercy
    and to walk humbly with your God.
                    Micah 6:8 NIV

What does "walking with God" mean to you?

_____

_____

_____

_____

**Read Micah 6:8 in a few different translations (using BibleGateway
.com or BibleStudyTools.com). How would you describe the three
things the Lord requires of us that are mentioned in this verse?
Why do you think these three in particular are mentioned?**

_____

_____

_____

_____

Micah was an Old Testament prophet who spoke to leaders and common people alike. He preached boldly against the social and ethical injustices of the time. When a wealthy merchant class was exploiting the poor farmers in Judah, Micah spoke against this injustice. Micah's message still applies to us today as God still cares deeply about the marginalized in society and expects us to do the same.[7]

Micah 6:8 is a summary of how God desires us to live. "To walk humbly with your God" means to move in step with God, to allow Him to set the pace and be our guide. If we are walking with God, we are marked by humility, not arrogance or pride.

We are also to "act justly and love mercy." Again, we see these two values of justice and mercy working in tandem. In this verse, the Hebrew word translated as "mercy" is *hesed*. Sound familiar? It's the same word from the book of Ruth that we studied in week 3.

The Hebrew word for justice is *mishpat*, meaning to treat people equitably. *Mishpat* puts emphasis on action, while *hesed* helps guide our attitudes and steer the motives behind our actions. As Timothy Keller writes, "To walk with God, then, we must do justice out of merciful love."[8]

Let's look at a few other examples of *mishpat* in the Bible. Read Zechariah 7:9–10 which is a call to justice and mercy just after King Darius allowed the Jewish people to return from exile in Babylon. How do these verses echo Micah 6:8?

Back on week 3, day 2, we talked about God's heart for the vulnerable. We learned how God makes a pathway of special provision for vulnerable groups throughout the Bible, especially but not limited to widows, orphans, immigrants, and the poor. Today we might expand this to include the refugee, the migrant worker, the pregnant teen, the homeless, the single parent, the divorced woman, the elderly, or the undocumented. As we have discovered through the Scriptures we've read this week, God asks that provision come through you and me. When we neglect to care for these vulnerable groups, it's not just a lack of mercy but also a violation of justice (*mishpat*).[9]

Read Psalm 146:5–9 in the English Standard Version. Circle the word *justice* in this passage and write the word *mishpat* in the margin next to it. Make a list of the people groups to whom God gives justice and mercy in these verses.

_____

_____

_____

_____

These verses remind me of Cherie, a widow friend who lives in Haiti. Her husband died more than a decade ago as a result of malnourishment and dehydration. She would often *tap-tap-tap* on the back screen door of the house built by my late husband Ericlee's grandparents in the northern mountains.

The first thing most people notice about Cherie is that she's blind. She would often bring one of her six children to guide her steps as she traveled the five miles on a dusty road to the mission house. Cherie's frail frame and gentle voice always stir up compassion in my heart.

I don't remember exactly when I first met Cherie, but during my twenty years of traveling and working in northern Haiti, she has shown up regularly. Somehow she always knows when I am in town.

In the early days, she would ask me for canned food to help feed her children. The cans were something they could carry on the long journey home to share with the others. I would dig through our cupboards and send her home with canned chicken or tuna and sometimes tomato paste or soup. She would down a glass of water and squeeze my hand before she left.

Widows in the country of Haiti are among the most vulnerable members of society. Cherie is just one of many widows who struggle to survive. Often they become homeless and outcasts when their husbands die. Few have extended family to care for them. While widows in the United States might have access to Social Security benefits, life insurance, or death benefits, no government programs provide for the needs of widows in Haiti.

When my husband Ericlee and I were first married, we talked a lot about God's heart for the vulnerable. Our own hearts were especially burdened for the orphans in Haiti. I remember one summer we looked up all the verses in the Bible that talked about orphans. What I didn't realize was important at that time is that most of the Scriptures that talk about caring for orphans also mention providing for widows.

It wasn't until my husband soared to heaven in 2014 that I returned to the Bible to investigate these passages that expressed God's heart for widows. As a young widow with three fatherless daughters, I wanted to remind myself what God said.

In 2019, when my family traveled back to Haiti for a women's conference, I visited a small church in the town of Fontaine pastored by my friend Gerby. He was especially excited for me to meet and encourage the widows in his church. That Sunday morning I got to hear the stories of several of these women.

Their grief and loss were familiar to me as a widow, yet the struggles they faced were so different. Jobs were hard to come by, so providing for their families was an enormous challenge. I learned that the church fed them a meal after the service and realized that this might be the only full meal some of them would enjoy for several days. I prayed and wept over my widow sisters.

Sitting on the end of the front pew that day was my friend Cherie. After our time of sharing, she rose, reached out for my hand, and clung to me. Pastor Gerby led us outside the church. He showed us the orphanage and school that were part of the campus. Then he began to illuminate his vision for building a widows home for these women in his church.

My heart was immediately moved by this vision. My new husband, Shawn, also felt the call to invest in this project. We were especially impressed that God and the local church were already moving in that direction. They were already feeding these women. Pastor Gerby also talked about how these women could be given jobs on the campus serving lunches to the schoolchildren, helping in the orphanage, or beautifying the church. They would have not only jobs but also a new sense of purpose and community.

When we returned to our home in California, we began raising funds for the widows home. This was a tangible way our family could leverage our connections and extend a hand of mercy to these widows in need. Out of our own grief and loss, God grew a passion for this specific project.

Read Acts 6:1–7. What is the conflict in the church at this time? How do they resolve this conflict and administer care for the widows in need?

We can learn about both justice and mercy from this situation in the early church. Justice was required for the widows who were being overlooked in the daily distribution of food. A new system needed to be put in place to care for them. This system included appointing seven men who were of good reputation, wise, and full of the Spirit. These men were chosen to oversee the care and financial needs of the widows. They needed mercy and compassion to assess those needs and provide for them.

> What are some examples of injustice you have seen in your own community? How could you be a part of bringing justice and mercy in those situations?

SCRIPTURE MEMORY MOMENT

Sometimes adding music and movement can help our memorization skills. Add a little rhythm as you practice Isaiah 30:18 by clapping along as you say it out loud.

A PRAYER FOR TODAY

DEAR JESUS, *impress upon my heart the injustices You want me to be sensitive about in my community. Connect me with real people and stories that will move my conviction into action. Give me courage to step out in new ways as You are creating a heart of mercy in me. Amen.*

Speak and act as those who are to be judged by the law of freedom. For judgment is without mercy to the one who has not shown mercy. Mercy triumphs over judgment.

What good is it, my brothers and sisters, if someone claims to have faith but does not have works? Can such faith save him?

If a brother or sister is without clothes and lacks daily food and one of you says to them, "Go in peace, stay warm, and be well fed," but you don't give them what the body needs, what good is it? In the same way faith, if it does not have works, is dead by itself.

James 2:12–17 CSB

What do you think is more important—faith or good works? Do you lean toward one or the other in your own life?

_____

_____

_____

_____

Today we are returning to the book of James to look at how justice and mercy work in tandem. This section of Scripture highlights the connection between faith and works. In James 2:12, James urges us to speak and act with the knowledge that we will stand before the judgment seat of God one day. He wants his audience to know that it is possible for a believer to have a useless faith. In other words, we can have a belief in God that is not backed by our actions or good works.[10]

Some people think James is contradicting Paul, who teaches that we are justified by faith alone. Let's dig into what Paul says on this topic.

Read Romans 3:21–31. How would you summarize what Paul is talking about in this passage?

_____

_____

_____

_____

Tony Evans explains, "Paul is talking about how a sinner becomes a saint, whereas James is talking about how a saint brings heaven to earth. You cannot merit salvation; it is received by grace through faith in Christ alone. Our sanctification, however, requires that our faith express itself in works."[11]

Look up the word _sanctification_ in the dictionary. Write down some definitions here. Based on these definitions, how do you think sanctification requires that our faith express itself in works?

_____

_____

_____

_____

The difference between salvation and sanctification is what allowed the repentant criminal on the cross beside Jesus to enter into heaven (Luke 23:39–43). His believing and repentant heart was his ticket to heaven. At that point, he didn't have time left to pursue good works. However, for those of us still on earth who believe in Jesus as our Savior, we have the opportunity to express our love for Him and mercy for others through compassionate deeds.

Sanctification is the process of maturing in our faith. As followers of Christ, we are moving toward holiness and righteousness even though we will not achieve them on earth. Theologians call this "progressive sanctification," because it's an ongoing process that lasts a lifetime. When we show mercy to others like Jesus has shown to us, it's part of the process. For example, if we give clothes or food to those in need, as James suggests, we learn about generosity. If we sacrifice some of our personal funds to sponsor a child or give toward disaster relief, then we can cultivate compassion. When mercy pushes us beyond our natural giving boundaries, God can sanctify our hearts. Of course, our ultimate sanctification will happen after death when God sets His people free from the presence and possibility of sin.

Read Ephesians 2:8–10. How does Paul define the relationship between faith and works?

Paul takes time to reiterate that we are saved by grace, not works. This levels the playing field. There's no spiritual scoreboard, no ranking or hierarchy among believers. We can't consider ourselves better than others if or when we do spiritual works. We can only brag about God's mercy and grace, which we receive and in turn offer to others.

> Considering what you learned today, what are some tangible ways you can allow mercy to season justice in your own life? Think about what this might look like with your spouse, while parenting your children, through friendships, as you interact with those who live in your neighborhood, and even in how you treat someone who has wronged you.

SCRIPTURE MEMORY MOMENT

Write out Isaiah 30:18 three times in your journal. As we move into the next week of our study, continue to reflect on these words.

When mercy pushes us beyond our natural giving boundaries, God can sanctify our hearts.

A PRAYER FOR TODAY

DEAR JESUS, *I am grateful for Your heart of justice and mercy. Continue to show me how to live out my faith through the good works You have prepared in advance for me to do. Sanctify my heart as You teach me to allow mercy to season justice in my life. Amen.*

HOW IS MERCY PART OF OUR PURPOSE?

Friend, you made it to the final week of the *Create in Me a Heart of Mercy* Bible study! I find it's always a little bittersweet when we draw to the close of a concentrated time of learning together. Of course, this is really just the beginning of our journey in learning to multiply mercy to the world. I'm so proud of you for persevering, digging into the deep places, and allowing God to cultivate the soil of your heart. I hope seeds have been planted along the way as you have explored examples of God's mercy throughout the Old and New Testaments.

In this final week, we will be looking at the stories of five people from the New Testament whose lives were transformed by God's mercy. Each of them in turn feels compelled to extend that mercy to others.

In today's opening story, (in)courage writer Rachel Marie Kang ushers us into that theme with a personal story about when she made a decision to receive God's mercy and pursue His purpose for her life. Pay attention to the way she was compelled to *live out* mercy after meeting God in a personal way. Ask God to show you specific ways you can live out mercy in your own life.

A Story of Mercy

I'll never forget where I was, how the hair on my arms stood straight up and goosebumps erupted all over my skin. I'll never forget how my pounding heart beat like a drum until I could hardly sit in my chair and found myself standing and walking to the front of the room with the rest of the teen girls, who were falling to their knees and breaking down in tears.

Just hours before, I had been laughing with my friends in our cabin, feeling fine and free. It wasn't supposed to be anything more than a summer camp—a time to make memories and have fun with friends. Never in a million years could I imagine I'd end up splitting my heart wide open, sitting on the floor of some big gathering room, and crying loudly with prayers pouring from my heart.

The speaker stood on the stage, telling her story and speaking of all the pain and sorrow she once held inside. As she spoke, she lugged around a ball and chain that was attached to her ankle. She told us that holding on to pain and hurt is like being shackled to a heavy weight that always follows and drags, and that the only way to be free of it is to forgive—both ourselves and others.

I thought about the pain I carried from watching my older brother live a life full of sickness and suffering. I thought about the pain I carried from watching my parents split and go their separate ways. I thought about the pain I carried from losing friends after moving from school to school to school. I thought about the sadness I cradled and how it had twisted into a bitter resentment that left me wondering why everything in my life always seemed to fall apart.

I sat on that floor with the rest of the teenagers spilling their hearts out, and I joined in. I joined not because I needed to do what everyone else was doing but because I needed to understand this God for myself. I needed to know if He really could hold my heart, heal my hurt, and set me free from the shackles of sorrow.

My prayer, a whirlwind of whispered words, came out slow and honest:

Dear God, I don't know who You are. I don't know if You're real. But if You are, please take my hurt and give me a heart that cares for others the way that You do. Give me eyes to see the world the way You do and a mouth to speak the way You speak.

When I got up from the floor that day, I didn't feel any different. I didn't feel changed or all charged up to go set the world on fire. I only hoped that God had heard me, that He would help me, and that He would have His way in my heart.

Not too long after this moment of sweet surrender, I traveled with my church to Quito, Ecuador, for a weeklong community outreach. Each night we sat under the big white tent as the same refrain played from a wonky keyboard and we all sang: *Gracias, gracias Señor. Gracias mi Señor, Jesus.* Hands lifting, voices rising in both English and Spanish, we sang this song about receiving the gift of everlasting mercy and everlasting life, about being set free through the blood of Jesus.

On my last day in Quito, I sat on the bleachers at the soccer field and wrapped a young girl in my sweater to shield her from the wind. As we sat there, watching the kids on the field kicking up dust for hours on end, I looked out at the horizon and found myself thinking back to that camp prayer I prayed.

It felt almost as if everything I'd ever felt had been released. I felt compassion—a desire to care about the pain of others—filling me up to overflow. And in that moment I realized that I couldn't care for the people of a capital city halfway around the world without caring for the people closest to me. I realized I didn't just want to receive the gift of mercy that I had been singing about. I wanted to extend mercy like God does. I wanted to *live* out mercy and I wanted to *give* mercy.

I felt like Saul (aka Paul) on the road to Damascus as he journeyed from merciless to merciful—from persecuting Christians to passionately proclaiming Christ. Found and forgiven, he was set free to unashamedly share the message of God's loving-kindness.

This is why mercy matters, because it spreads like wildfire and burns bright with redemption. Mercy restores us to one another while also restoring us to God. And that is God's heart—that none of us would be far from love or far from Him.

And what a gift it is that His mercy is not just for today. It stretches into tomorrow, saves and secures us even for life after life. Mercy sets us free not just here on earth but for eternity.

The thought of such grace sends chills down my spine.

—RACHEL MARIE KANG

Have you had a time in your life when the weight of circumstances, doubt, or unforgiveness dragged you down? Did you invite God into it? If so, how did His presence help?

Read the story of Saul's conversion in Acts 9:1–19. How was his life transformed and what was the specific purpose Jesus appointed him to?

Saul had been breathing out threats and murder against God's people. He actually requested letters from the high priest that he could present to the synagogues in Damascus giving him permission to track down Christ followers and take them to Jerusalem for punishment. Strategically located 150 miles northeast of Jerusalem, Damascus was an important ancient city and commercial center where caravans converged. Because a large Jewish population lived in Damascus, Saul recognized that Christianity could spread from Damascus throughout the world.

Saul positioned himself as kind of a religious bounty hunter to put a stop to those who were followers of the Way and ultimately to halt the spread of the gospel. "The Way" was an early term used in reference to Christianity because Jesus proclaimed He was "the way, and the truth, and the life" (John 14:6).

In Acts 26, Paul retells his conversion experience to King Agrippa in an effort to persuade him to believe in Jesus. Read how Paul recalls what Jesus told him on the road to Damascus:

> And I said, "Who are you, Lord?" And the Lord said, "I am Jesus whom you are persecuting. But rise and stand upon your feet, for I have appeared to you for this purpose, to appoint you as a servant and witness to the things in which you have seen me and to those in which I will appear to you, delivering you from your people and from the Gentiles—to whom I am sending you to open their eyes, so that they may turn from darkness to light and from the power of Satan to God, that they may receive forgiveness of sins and a place among those who are sanctified by faith in me." (vv. 15–18)

Jesus unites Himself with the church through these words. He feels the persecution against the church in a personal way, and He chooses to identify with their pain and enter into it.[1] When Jesus confronts Paul, He clearly states His purpose to appoint Paul as His servant and witness to the gentiles.

Paul was a "chosen instrument" of God (Acts 9:15). His original purpose was to harm the Christian believers, but God's purpose for him was actually to multiply the believers and prove that Jesus was the Christ. Today we know Paul as one of the greatest missionaries in history who wrote most of the New Testament epistles, planted numerous churches, and worked side by side with Peter and John and the other apostles.

Paul's life is a beautiful example of the mercy of God. After the way he persecuted the early Jewish believers in Jesus, he certainly didn't deserve forgiveness or kindness. Still, Paul is chosen by God and his life is transformed after meeting Jesus on the road to Damascus. His story doesn't stop there. He is sent out to multiply God's mercy, sharing the message of God's generous love and compassion with others, especially with gentiles and kings. Paul's transformation is part of his witness.

When we share our stories of transformation with others, we can point them to God's mercy. We can do that in all sorts of ways. It doesn't have to be through preaching or planting churches like Paul (although it certainly could be!). God can use our stories to influence our children, spouses, neighbors, or friends. He might call us to write a children's book, to volunteer and serve meals to the homeless, to start a podcast sharing other people's stories, to teach a class or lead a small group, or to share a bit of our own story of mercy with someone in line at the coffee shop.

In the same way that Paul was chosen by God, you are chosen too. What does it mean to you that you are chosen by God to multiply mercy to others?

SCRIPTURE MEMORY MOMENT

This week's memory passage is Luke 4:18–19. In week 3, we read the passage from Isaiah 61 that is referenced here. This is a significant moment in the New Testament when Jesus enters the synagogue in His hometown of Nazareth and stands up to read. The scroll of the prophet Isaiah is handed to Him, and He reads these words as a way of proclaiming His purpose for ministry. Read through these two verses and underline the key phrases. Begin to memorize the first sentence.

> *The Spirit of the Lord is upon me,*
> *because he has anointed me*
> *to proclaim good news to the poor.*
> *He has sent me to proclaim liberty to the captives*
> *and recovering of sight to the blind,*
> *to set at liberty those who are oppressed,*
> *to proclaim the year of the Lord's favor.*

A PRAYER FOR TODAY

DEAR FATHER, *thank You for these stories of lives transformed by Your mercy. I long to be continually transformed by Your mercy in my life as well. Thank You for choosing me to multiply Your message of mercy. Show me creative ways that I might do that. Amen.*

DAY 2

Now there was at Joppa a certain disciple named Tabitha, which when translated, means Dorcas. This woman was full of good works and acts of mercy which she did.

Acts 9:36 WEB

Who is someone in your life, your church, or your community known for her good works or acts of charity? Describe that person.

_____

_____

_____

_____

Read Acts 9:36–42 to get a fuller picture of Dorcas's story. Write down any significant details about her and her service that you learn from this passage.

_____

_____

_____

_____

Dorcas (also called Tabitha) was a disciple known by her good works and specifically her heart for widows. You may recall from our study of

> *This* is why mercy matters, because it spreads like wildfire and burns bright with redemption. Mercy restores us to one another while also restoring us to God.
>
> —RACHEL MARIE KANG

Ruth that widows were a vulnerable group of people in ancient culture. If widows didn't have any male heirs to care for them, they struggled to find a livelihood and were often taken advantage of and left destitute.

Dorcas lived in Joppa, the main seaport serving Jerusalem. Because of the dangerous nature of working and traveling on the water, a maritime community probably would have had more widows and orphans than other areas. These verses in Acts describe a woman who cares for widows and others in practical ways. Service is a natural expression of her merciful heart. She uses her domestic talents, including sewing clothes, to serve those in need.[2]

Dorcas is an example of how small acts of mercy can have a big impact. Her influence was widespread and long-lasting because she put others first in her life. Clearly, God is not done with her yet. Through Peter, God performs a miracle that restores her from death to life.

> **Write out Galatians 6:2. What do you think it means to "bear one another's burdens"?**
>
> _____
>
> _____
>
> _____
>
> _____

This verse is part of the apostle Paul's closing exhortations to the churches in the southern area of Galatia. He was concerned that the

Galatians were deserting the gospel he had preached to them because a number of prominent Jewish legalists had infiltrated the congregation. They were teaching that faith in Christ alone was not enough to make a person right with God. Paul drives home that they do not need to earn their salvation in any way, but that part of fulfilling the "law of Christ"—or the law of love—is in bearing one another's burdens.[3]

We can bear or carry each other's burdens in a variety of ways. Dorcas chooses to serve in tangible ways behind the scenes to help bear the burdens of others. She comes alongside the grieving widows by tending to their physical needs and making them clothes. She uses the work of her hands to show kindness and care to these women.

When Ericlee died from cancer, my daughters and I were blessed by an abundance of acts of mercy from our community. Many friends walked alongside us in our grief in practical ways—helping with laundry, washing dishes, fixing things in our home, taking care of my car maintenance, and even helping decorate our Christmas tree. People brought us meals and sent gift cards that sustained us for months.

I remember going to an eye doctor, whose phone number I found online, only to discover upon arrival that my late husband had been a teacher and coach to the optometrist's daughter. He gifted me the examination and the contact lenses I needed. And God showed me again His special and creative provision for widows and their children.

Think of someone in your life whom God might be calling you to share provision with today. Write down some ideas of what you might do to serve them.

When Dorcas becomes sick and dies in Acts 9:37, the widows and others in her community mourn deeply. Dorcas had grieved with them and served them, and now they grieve losing her. It just so happens that the apostle Peter is nearby in a town called Lydda. Some of the disciples send for Peter and urge him to come to the home of Dorcas.

When Peter arrives, a group of widows are gathered at the house, weeping and grieving the loss of their friend. Peter asks everyone to step outside, and then he kneels to pray. He addresses the dead woman by name, saying, "Tabitha, arise," and she opens her eyes and sits up. Peter helps her to stand and presents her alive to the others.

This is the first time one of the apostles has raised someone from death to life like Jesus did. These miracles were performed not for shock value but to draw more people to Christ. Dorcas had mercifully served others, and then God showed her miraculous mercy by extending her life.[4]

Galatians 6:9 says, "So let's not get tired of doing what is good. At just the right time we will reap a harvest of blessing if we don't give up" (NLT). Dorcas lived a life that was filled with examples of doing good, as evidenced by the many people who mourned her death. She was not merely checking boxes or trying to gain notoriety. Rather, her good deeds were an overflow of the kindness and mercy she'd received from her Savior. Her life pointed others toward the true source of mercy: Jesus and His life, death, and resurrection.

Read Matthew 6:1–4. How do these verses describe the way Dorcas served?

Even our hidden works to help those in need do not go unnoticed. Dorcas does not show off her skills, nor does she bury her talents. She works diligently and quietly to serve the needs of others in her community. She values the widows and gives them hope just as Jesus had offered her new life and hope.

As Rachel shared in this week's opening story, *this* is why mercy matters. "Mercy restores us to one another while also restoring us to God. And that is God's heart—that none of us would be far from love or far from Him." Amen.

SCRIPTURE MEMORY MOMENT

Take a walk in your neighborhood or on a nearby trail and work on memorizing Luke 4:18–19. Fresh air and movement can help us in the process of memorization.

A PRAYER FOR TODAY

DEAR GOD, *thank You for all the practical and creative ways You provide for our needs. Today I'm grateful for the story of Dorcas. Reveal to me tangible ways I can show mercy and serve the people around me like she did. Purify my heart and my motives so I can serve others with gladness. Amen.*

After this Paul left Athens and went to Corinth. And he found a Jew named Aquila, a native of Pontus, recently come from Italy with his wife Priscilla, because Claudius had commanded all the Jews to leave Rome. And he went to see them, and because he was of the same trade he stayed with them and worked, for they were tentmakers by trade.

Acts 18:1–3

What does the word *purpose* mean to you? How would you describe your life purpose?

_____

_____

_____

_____

This week we are digging into the stories of five people from the New Testament who embraced mercy as part of their purpose. We've already learned about Paul and Dorcas. Today we are going to learn about Priscilla, a woman whose story is sprinkled throughout the pages of the New Testament. Along with her husband, Aquila, and the apostle Paul, Priscilla stepped into an important role of leadership and helped build the early church.

Read Acts 18:1–3. What do you learn about Priscilla and Aquila from these verses? What do they have in common with Paul, and why might that be significant?

_____

_____

_____

_____

Priscilla and Aquila had been forced to leave Rome when Emperor Claudius expelled all Jews from the city in AD 49. They ended up in Corinth, a city located along important trade routes with access to several port cities. Meanwhile, Paul had left Athens and traveled to Corinth, knowing it was a strategic city where he could share the gospel.

When Paul first meets Priscilla and Aquila, he decides to stay with them and work together with them since they are tentmakers. Tentmaking was Paul's day job that paid the bills and allowed him to follow his true purpose and calling—persuading both Jews and gentiles to believe in and follow Christ. This turns out to be the perfect collaboration. Paul stays with Priscilla and Aquila and eventually recruits them to help with building the church.

Part of God's mercy is including people like Paul, Dorcas, Priscilla, Aquila, you, and me in the work of building His kingdom. We don't deserve it. He could certainly do it without us. But He chooses to give each of us specific roles and callings to participate in His kingdom work. We get to taste His glory when we serve in our callings. His mercy is including us!

In his book *Unfinished*, Richard Stearns, president of World Vision, writes that we will never find our deepest purpose in life until we find our place in building God's kingdom. "We all have the same general assignment but our specific roles within it will be unique to us as individuals and will take into account our gifts and talents but also our experience, our assets, our physical location, and our connections and associations."[5]

Think about it: Priscilla and Aquila had been forced to leave their home in Rome and relocate. We don't get all the details in the text, but we can imagine that was a hardship. Whenever you have to move to a new place, you must navigate grief and transition. Moving often means reevaluating, recalibrating, and building new relationships. Despite its challenges, that move allowed Priscilla and Aquila to cross paths with Paul. This ended up being beneficial for all of them and was the pathway to their calling in God's kingdom.

Have you ever experienced an unplanned or even unwanted move from a house, a job, or a church? How did that move open new doors for you to pursue a new sense of purpose?

Priscilla and Aquila spent a lot of time with Paul. They worked together, learned together, did ministry together, and even traveled together. Read the following verses. How was God using them? What do these events and details show about Priscilla and Aquila's calling in God's kingdom?

Acts 18:18–21
Acts 18:24–28
Romans 16:3–5
1 Corinthians 16:19

———————————————————————————

———————————————————————————

Priscilla and Aquila are co-laborers for Christ alongside Paul. In their tentmaking and their work spreading the good news of Jesus, Paul recognizes their work ethic and commitment to the gospel. Acts 18:20–21 says Paul leaves the couple in Ephesus, trusting them to lead the church plant there.

When we talk about the church in the New Testament period, we are not talking about a physical church building or attending a service with a worship band, a preacher, and donuts in the fellowship hall. Priscilla and Aquila would have hosted the church in their own home and led the group as well. Their hospitality was paramount to their ministry. This may be one of the reasons Paul trusted them to lead. He had been the recipient of their hospitality and witnessed how they extended mercy to others.

Paul trained Priscilla and Aquila in teaching the gospel before setting them free to lead on their own. We see evidence of their training in the passage we read from Acts 18:24–28. When a passionate young preacher named Apollos arrives in Ephesus, they take time to mentor him. Apollos is articulate and persuasive, but he does not clearly understand the whole gospel. Priscilla and Aquila take him aside and gently correct him in private, showing their own humility and mercy toward him. They train Apollos as a brother in the faith so he can preach more accurately.

The place God calls you to is the place where your deep gladness and the world's deep hunger meet.

—FREDERICK BUECHNER

Priscilla takes hold of her purpose to help other believers grow in their faith and knowledge of God, working in partnership with her husband. Priscilla is a beautiful example of how God's mercy changes us and gives us new purpose. Theologian Frederick Buechner once wrote, "The place God calls you to is the place where your deep gladness and the world's deep hunger meet."[6] We see this in Priscilla and how she chooses to use her influence, gifts, and strengths.

Whether you are a barista at a coffee shop, a preschool teacher, a small business owner, a grandma who loves to garden, or a mom who writes poetry in the cracks of time, you were designed with a purpose. Maybe you have the gift of administration or preaching, or perhaps a heart for orphans or refugees. In that place where your passion and compassion meet, you have an opportunity to multiply mercy by loving others the way God has loved you.

> Read Colossians 3:23–24. How does the idea of working with God as your boss shift your sense of purpose? Jot down some ideas of how God might be calling you to use your gifts and talents in this present season.

SCRIPTURE MEMORY MOMENT

Write out Luke 4:18–19 on an index card or sticky note. Post it somewhere in your home where you will see it often, such as a bathroom mirror or on the refrigerator, so you can work on memorizing it regularly.

A PRAYER FOR TODAY

DEAR JESUS, *I am grateful for stories like Priscilla's where I can see You using a woman as a leader. Please shine a light on the gifts, talents, strengths, and even weaknesses I have that You might use for Your kingdom purpose. Remind me of the ways You have shown me mercy so I can multiply that mercy to others. Amen.*

And on the Sabbath day we went outside the gate to the riverside, where we supposed there was a place of prayer, and we sat down and spoke to the women who had come together. One who heard us was a woman named Lydia, from the city of Thyatira, a seller of purple goods, who was a worshiper of God. The Lord opened her heart to pay attention to what was said by Paul.

And after she was baptized, and her household as well, she urged us, saying, "If you have judged me to be faithful to the Lord, come to my house and stay." And she prevailed upon us.

Acts 16:13–15

Who do you know with the gift of hospitality? How have they extended hospitality to you?

Read Acts 16:13–15, where Luke, who was Paul's traveling companion, records the conversion of a woman named Lydia. What details do you learn about Lydia from these few verses?

Lydia's story serves as an example of how the gospel was spreading to new areas and how God in His mercy calls people from all walks of life to build His kingdom. Paul is traveling throughout Macedonia, Achaia, and Asia at this point in his missionary journey. He meets Lydia down by the river in Philippi, a Roman colony in Macedonia.

Lydia was a businesswoman from the city of Thyatira, which was in the Roman province of Lydda in Asia Minor and was known for its production of purple dye and dyed goods. We learn from the text that Lydia was a "dealer in purple cloth," a product that was extremely expensive and was purchased only by royalty and people of wealth.[7] In other words, Lydia had connections and resources.

With careful reading, we learn that Lydia worships and fears God but doesn't know the full picture of the gospel. The passage tells us that "the Lord opened her heart to pay attention to what was said by Paul" (Acts 16:14). This detail shows the way God was actively working in this situation and how His mercy brings another daughter into His family. When Lydia hears Paul share the good news about Jesus—His death, resurrection, and forgiveness of sins—she becomes a true believer. In fact, she becomes the first recorded convert to Christianity in Europe.

Let's lean into the text to see what Lydia does after she makes a decision to believe in Jesus: "After she was baptized, and her household as well" (Acts 16:15). Immediately after believing in Jesus, Lydia decides to get baptized. (After all, they were down by the river, so why not?!) Lydia then proceeds to lead her entire household—including her servants and any family members old enough to comprehend—to believe in Jesus Christ and get baptized as well. God's mercy extends not just to Lydia but to her entire clan. As Rachel wrote in this week's opening story, "Mercy sets us free not just here on earth but for eternity."

How is Lydia compelled by God's mercy to extend mercy to others?

_____

_____

_____

_____

After sharing her newfound belief with those closest to her, Lydia then uses her gift of hospitality and invites Paul to stay with her. Her home eventually becomes the base of operations for the church in Philippi. She is a prime example of a woman who uses her gifts of hospitality, leadership, and influence for God's glory.

Hospitality at its basic level is generous and gracious treatment of guests, and it's one way we can show the kindness of God to others. I love hosting Bible study groups, my daughter's track and field team, friends passing through town, our moms prayer group from school, and our church life group (four families who meet regularly at our place for Sunday supper and prayer time). Making them feel welcome and cared for allows me to pass on the mercy God has shown me.

Food is my love language, and nourishing people well at my table is a gift. Whether it's cooking up an Italian meal using my mama's manicotti recipe or grilling burgers and veggies, it's important to me that food is abundant and people feel welcome. Through food, I can make people feel special and loved in the same way God reminds me that I'm wonderfully made and completely adored. Filling their bellies and gathering at our table opens opportunities for meaningful conversations about hurts, hardships, and faith—something that might not happen if we stayed in a less comfortable or more formal setting.

Although it often involves opening one's home, hospitality doesn't have to look a certain way. You don't have to serve up fancy food or have a big house. You can take food on the road and bless people by delivering meals after they have a new baby or when they are sick or have buried a loved one. Hospitality is our opportunity to respond to God's mercy by offering kindness and tender care to others.

Pastor and author Rich Villodas describes hospitality as a value of opening our hearts. In his book *The Deeply Formed Life*, he writes, "The deeply formed life is one that creates space for others. Whether that space is at our work right in our own cubicles, with families at parks, or through opening our home to others, we cannot be deeply formed into the image of Jesus without our lives mirroring gracious hospitality."[8]

Lydia opened her heart to the gospel and her whole family received God's mercy. She in turn opened her home to the Philippi community, and many others had a space to form and grow in their faith.

> **What are some ways you can extend hospitality to people in your community today?**

Biblical hospitality is often an invitation to rest. Abraham models this in Genesis 18 when three strangers show up during the hottest part of the day and he invites them inside his tent. Abraham said, "If it pleases you, stop here for a while. Rest in the shade of this tree while water is brought to wash your feet" (Gen. 18:3–4 NLT).

Abraham provides for these travelers by greeting them warmly, giving them water to wash their feet, and offering nourishing food and a place to rest. He didn't know it at the time, but these weary travelers were actually angels (and some scholars believe one of them may have been the preincarnate Christ, "the LORD"). Once they have been made comfortable and are fed, these visitors announce that Abraham and Sarah will have a son within the next year. That promised child, Isaac, was a gift of mercy to Abraham and Sarah. They did nothing to deserve or earn a child, but God in His mercy sends a son to fulfill His promise to them.

Hebrews 13:2 reminds us, "Don't forget to show hospitality to strangers, for some who have done this have entertained angels without realizing it!" (NLT). Who can you extend hospitality to by inviting them into your home or out for a cup of coffee? Maybe God has given you a home that has a guest room or a bigger yard where you can host a Bible study. Perhaps hospitality looks like inviting someone to sit next to you in class or striking up a conversation with someone on the bus. Whatever it looks like for you, consider allowing God to open your heart through hospitality as His mercy overflows to those around you.

> **Read 1 Peter 4:8–10. In light of these verses, how can we make hospitality genuine? How does today's study shape your perspective on hospitality?**

SCRIPTURE MEMORY MOMENT

Practice Luke 4:18–19 by writing it out on a piece of paper. If you want to get creative, add pictures or use a different kind of lettering that will help remind you of key words.

A PRAYER FOR TODAY

DEAR JESUS, *I'm humbled by the way You extended mercy and hospitality to me through Your sacrifice on the cross. Thank You for welcoming me into Your family when I didn't deserve it. I'm longing to show hospitality to others like Lydia did. Open my heart and the doors of opportunity. Amen.*

Six days before the Passover, Jesus therefore came to Bethany, where Lazarus was, whom Jesus had raised from the dead. So they gave a dinner for him there. Martha served, and Lazarus was one of those reclining with him at table. Mary therefore took a pound of expensive ointment made from pure nard, and anointed the feet of Jesus and wiped his feet with her hair. The house was filled with the fragrance of the perfume. But Judas Iscariot, one of his disciples (he who was about to betray him), said, "Why was this ointment not sold for three hundred denarii and given to the poor?" He said this, not because he cared about the poor, but because he was a thief, and having charge of the moneybag he used to help himself to what was put into it. Jesus said, "Leave her alone, so that she may keep it for the day of my burial. For the poor you always have with you, but you do not always have me."

John 12:1–8

Describe something you own or have been given that is of great value. What makes it so valuable to you?

Read Luke 10:38–42. These verses introduce two sisters, Mary and Martha, who are dear friends to Jesus. Even if you are familiar with this story, pay particular attention to the descriptions of these two sisters. How would you characterize each of them?

Mary

_____

_____

Martha

_____

_____

Although both of these women have hearts to serve, this plays out in different ways for each of them. Martha serves perhaps in more traditional ways that were expected of women in ancient Jewish culture—by cooking, cleaning, and welcoming people into her home. Yet Jesus commends Mary for her focused devotion to learning from and listening to him. It's not that Martha's service is wrong or bad but that she is anxious and distracted from the Savior.

Reread the story in John 12:1–8. What words would you use to describe Mary's act of service to Jesus?

_____

_____

_____

_____

Mary knows she has been shown much mercy by Jesus. He is her teacher, inviting her to listen to His teaching at a time when women were not usually allowed access to teaching. He is her savior, the trusted friend who had grieved with her and the one who had raised her brother, Lazarus, from the grave (see John 11). Mary offers a profound act of sacrifice and humility in this scene. She takes an expensive ointment made from pure nard, which was worth more than a year's wages, to anoint Jesus. We do not know all the details of Mary's situation, but there is no mention of her being married. This perfume might have been her savings or her dowry for the future.

Imagine the scene with me: Jesus's feet would have been dirty and dusty from all the walking He did on the road. Washing someone's feet was a job the servants did as guests entered the house. Yet Mary chose to let down her hair—which Jewish women usually wore up or braided—and use it like a cloth to clean Jesus's feet. A woman's hair is her glory (1 Cor. 11:15), but Mary lays down her glory to elevate God's glory.

Mary shows her own humility by pouring this costly perfume over Jesus's feet instead of on His head, which would have been more customary. His mercy compels her to stoop low, to give of herself. This act is symbolic of preparing a body for burial. In his Gospel, John points out the significance that this occurred six days before the Passover. Jesus's burial was only a few days away.

Judas, the disciple who was about to betray Jesus, challenges Mary's actions and asks, "Why was this ointment not sold for three hundred denarii and given to the poor?" (John 12:5). Of course, he doesn't really care about the poor, as the text reveals. Rather, he's looking out for his own financial gain. Judas seems to suggest that Jesus is not worthy of this extravagant display, but Mary recognizes that Jesus is her Savior and the only one truly deserving of such an offering.

Because of the mercy Jesus has shown her, Mary is compelled to honor Him in this moment. Mary is so overcome with gratitude and love that she is moved to an extreme gesture of kindness. She

Whether you are a mama, grandma, auntie, or mentor, married, widowed, or single, you have the opportunity to model God's mercy for others today.

illustrates her overflowing heart by pouring out her precious perfume. When Judas questions her actions, Jesus defends Mary publicly and even says that she kept this perfume for the day of His burial.

Take some time to reflect on what Mary did for Jesus. She is remembered for responding to Jesus with a radical display of love and devotion. Write out a prayer expressing your own response to Jesus for what He has done for you.

Friend, our time together is coming to a close. My prayer is that these last six weeks have given you a deeper understanding of mercy and how it is a character quality of God Himself. We have studied how mercy intersects with God's grace, kindness, faithfulness, justice, charity, and love.

Let's look to Jesus as our example of mercy and continue to seek out ways we can multiply mercy to others. Whether you are a mama, grandma, auntie, or mentor, married, widowed, or single, you have the opportunity to model God's mercy for others today. What a beautiful and high calling in His kingdom!

Take a few minutes to page through our study and remember some of the highlights or challenges you have experienced in these stories and lessons. What is one takeaway for you as you close the pages of this workbook? How will you move out in mercy?

Read these words aloud as a benediction (closing blessing) on what you have studied. May God continue to create a heart of mercy in you, my friend.

> Praise be to the God and Father of our Lord Jesus Christ! In his great mercy he has given us new birth into a living hope through the resurrection of Jesus Christ from the dead, and into an inheritance that can never perish, spoil or fade. This inheritance is kept in heaven for you, who through faith are shielded by God's power until the coming of the salvation that is ready to be revealed in the last time. (1 Pet. 1:3–5 NIV)

SCRIPTURE MEMORY MOMENT

Take some time to share Luke 4:18–19 with a friend, a spouse, or a child. Explain why this passage is meaningful to you after this study of mercy. Friend, I'm so proud of you! You have joined me in meditating on and memorizing these six different Scriptures about mercy. Take some time to look back over them and let them encourage your heart.

A PRAYER FOR TODAY

DEAR FATHER, *You are the God of mercy. You have done so many amazing things to show You love me. Make me like Mary—willing to humbly pour out in sacrifice to You and to others. Continue to break my heart for the things that break Your heart and to create in me a heart of mercy. Amen.*

NOTES

Week 1 What Is Mercy?

1. *Easton's Bible Dictionary*, s.v. "mercy," Blue Letter Bible, https://www.blueletter
bible.org/search/dictionary/viewtopic.cfm?topic=ET0002494.

2. Lawrence O. Richards, *Expository Dictionary of Bible Words*, s.v. "mercy" (Grand
Rapids: Zondervan, 1985), 440.

3. Tara-Leigh Cobble, *The Bible Recap* (Minneapolis: Bethany House, 2020), 50.

4. Seth J. Gillihan, "The Healing Power of Telling Your Trauma Story," Psychology
Today, March 6, 2019, https://www.psychologytoday.com/us/blog/think-act-be/201903
/the-healing-power-telling-your-trauma-story.

5. Tony Evans, note on Exodus 34:6–7, *Tony Evans Study Bible* (Nashville: Holman,
2017), 107.

6. Shadia Hrichi, *Hagar: Rediscovering the God Who Sees Me* (Abilene, TX: Leaf-
wood Publishers, 2017), 133.

Week 2 Why Do We Need Mercy?

1. Philip Wijaya, "What Is the Difference Between Grace and Mercy?," Christianity
.com, July 8, 2019, https://www.christianity.com/wiki/christian-terms/what-is-the
-difference-between-grace-and-mercy.html.

2. Mitchel Lee, *Even If: Trusting God When Life Disappoints, Overwhelms, or Just
Doesn't Make Sense* (Colorado Springs: Multnomah, 2021), 6.

3. Abigail Cook, "Transactional Relationships in Psychology: Definition & Examples," Study.com, January 26, 2021, https://study.com/academy/lesson/transactional
-relationships-in-psychology-definition-examples.html.

4. David Platt, "Miraculous Mercy," *Radical Podcast*, May 13, 2012, https://radical
.net/podcast/miraculous-mercy/.

5. Tara-Leigh Cobble, *The Bible Recap* (Minneapolis: Bethany House, 2020), 694–95.

6. *Merriam-Webster*, s.v. "chosen," accessed September 22, 2021, https://www
.merriam-webster.com/dictionary/chosen.

Week 3 How Do We Receive Mercy?

1. Carolyn Custis James, *The Gospel of Ruth: Loving God Enough to Break the Rules*
(Grand Rapids: Zondervan, 2008), 62.

2. Timothy Keller, *Generous Justice* (New York: Dutton, 2010), 4.

3. James, *The Gospel of Ruth*, 115.

4. James, *The Gospel of Ruth*, 51.

5. Carolyn Custis James, *Finding God in the Margins* (Bellingham, WA: Lexham Press, 2018), 52–55.

6. Paul Helm, "Providence," The Gospel Coalition, accessed August 16, 2021, https://www.thegospelcoalition.org/essay/providence/.

7. James, *The Gospel of Ruth*, 128–29.

8. Melanie Pinola, "The Science of Memory: Top 10 Proven Techniques to Remember More and Learn Faster," Zapier, June 6, 2019, https://zapier.com/blog/better-memory/.

9. R. Jamieson, A. R. Fausset, and David Brown, *Commentary Critical and Explanatory on the Whole Bible*, vol. 1 (Oak Harbor, WA: Logos Research Systems, Inc., 1997), 173.

10. John D. Barry et al., *Faithlife Study Bible* (Bellingham, WA: Lexham Press, 2016), notes on Ruth 3:1.

11. Saundra Dalton-Smith, *Sacred Rest: Recover Your Life, Renew Your Energy, Restore Your Sanity* (New York: Faith Words, 2017), 141.

Week 4 How Can We Extend Mercy in Our Everyday Lives?

1. Jackie Hill Perry, *Jude: Contending for the Faith in Today's Culture* (Nashville: Lifeway Press, 2020), 142–43.

2. Perry, *Jude*, 142–43.

3. Nikita Stewart, "I've Been to the Mountaintop. Dr. King's Last Sermon Annotated," *New York Times*, April 2, 2018, https://www.nytimes.com/interactive/2018/04/02/us/king-mlk-last-sermon-annotated.html.

4. Vivian Mabuni, *Open Hands, Willing Heart* (New York: Waterbrook, 2019), 165.

Week 5 How Do Mercy and Justice Coexist?

1. Matt Mikalatos, *Journey to Love: What We Long For, How to Find It, and How to Pass It On* (Carol Stream, IL: NavPress, 2021), 61.

2. Tony Evans, note on Ephesians 2:10–11, *Tony Evans Study Bible* (Nashville: Holman Bibles, 2017), 1473.

3. Ken Wytsma, *Pursuing Justice: The Call to Live and Die for Bigger Things* (Nashville: Thomas Nelson, 2013), 11.

4. Timothy Keller, *Generous Justice: How God's Grace Makes Us Just* (New York: Dutton, 2010), 83.

5. Tara-Leigh Cobble, *The Bible Recap* (Minneapolis: Bethany House, 2020), 636.

6. Cobble, *The Bible Recap*, 652.

7. Introduction to the book of Micah, *(in)courage Devotional Bible*, ed. Denise J. Hughes (Nashville: Holman Bibles, 2018), 1249.

8. Keller, *Generous Justice*, 3–4.

9. Keller, *Generous Justice*, 5.

10. Tony Evans, notes on James 2:12 and 2:14, *Tony Evans Study Bible* (Nashville: Holman Bibles, 2017), 1473.

11. Evans, note on James 2:14, *Tony Evans Study Bible*, 1473.

Week 6 How Is Mercy Part of Our Purpose?

1. Tara-Leigh Cobble, *The Bible Recap* (Minneapolis: Bethany House, 2020), 664.

2. Ethel L. Herr, *Chosen Women of the Bible* (Chicago: Moody, 1976), 82–85.

3. "The Book of Micah," (*in*)*courage Devotional Bible*, ed. Denise J. Hughes (Nashville: Holman Bibles, 2018), 1249.

4. Tony Evans, notes on Acts 9:32–35 and 9:40, *Tony Evans Study Bible* (Nashville: Holman Bibles, 2017), 1284.

5. Richard Stearns, *Unfinished: Believing Is Only the Beginning* (Nashville: Thomas Nelson, 2013), 131.

6. Frederick Buechner, "Vocation," FrederickBuechner.com, July 18, 2021, https://www.frederickbuechner.com/quote-of-the-day/2021/7/18/vocation.

7. "Meet Lydia, a Woman of Leadership," (*in*)*courage Devotional Bible* (Nashville: Holman Bibles, 2018), 1551.

8. Rich Villodas, *The Deeply Formed Life: Five Transformative Values to Root Us in the Way of Jesus* (Colorado Springs: Waterbrook, 2020), 196.

ABOUT THE AUTHORS

Dorina Lazo Gilmore-Young is an author, podcaster, speaker, and Bible teacher who loves to help people discover God's glory on life's unexpected trails. Dorina has published children's books, including *Cora Cooks Pancit* and *Chasing God's Glory*, Bible studies, poetry, and a devotional, *Walk Run Soar*. She lives in Central California with her hubby Shawn and three courageous daughters. Connect with Dorina at www.DorinaGilmore.com and on Instagram @DorinaGilmore.

Lucretia Berry is the founder of Brownicity, an agency committed to making important, scholarly, informed anti-racism education accessible. A former college professor, she has authored *Hues of You—An Activity Book for Learning About the Skin You Are In* and *What LIES Between Us—Fostering First Steps Toward Racial Healing*. Lucretia is married to Nathan; they have three daughters and two Aussiedoodles. Learn more from Lucretia at brownicity.com or on Instagram @lucretiaberry.

Simi John was born in India and raised in Texas. She is married to Jayson, who serves as a lead pastor at a local church, and they have two children. Simi is a speaker and author. Her passion is to empower women to walk confidently in their God-given identity. Connect with Simi at www.SimiJohn.tv and on Instagram @simijohn.

Rachel Marie Kang is a writer of prose, poems, and other pieces. She is the author of *Let There Be Art*, and her writing has been featured in *Christianity Today*, *Charlotte Magazine*, and at (in)courage. Rachel lives and writes from North Carolina at rachelmariekang.com and on Instagram @rachelmariekang.

Michelle Ami Reyes, PhD, is an author and activist. She received the 2022 ECPA Christian Book Award for New Author for her book *Becoming All Things*. Michelle writes at the intersection of multiculturalism, faith, and justice. She lives with her family in Austin, Texas. Connect with her at www.MichelleAmiReyes.com and on Instagram @michelleamireyes.

Renee Swope is a Word-lover, heart-encourager, and grace-needer. The bestselling author of *A Confident Heart* and her new release, *A Confident Mom*, Renee is a mom of two grown sons and a tweenage daughter. She loves gardening, making memories with her family, and creating beautiful spaces in her home. Find her at reneeswope.com and on social media @reneeswope.

(in)courage welcomes you

to an online community of women who seek Jesus together. Each weekday we meet you right where you are, as one of our thirty writers shares what's going on in her everyday life and how God's right in the middle of it all. They bring their unique experiences—joys and struggles equally—so that you can feel less alone and be empowered by the hope Jesus gives.

Learn more and join the sisterhood at **incourage.me** and connect with us on social media **@incourage**.

How to Delight in Differences, Love through Disagreements, and Live with Discomfort

In *Come Sit with Me*, more than two dozen (in)courage writers help you navigate tough relational tensions by revealing their own hard-fought, grace-filled learning moments. Whether you're in the middle of a conflict without resolution or wondering how to enter into a friend's pain, this book will serve as the guide you need to move through challenges and grow closer to God.